Copyright© One White's Pond Press
All rights reserved. No part of this publication may be reproduced, distributed, or transmitted in any form or by any means, including photocopying, recording, or other electronic or mechanical methods, without the prior written permission of the publisher, except in the case of brief quotations used in reviews or scholarly articles.

For permission requests, contact:
One White's Pond Press
In partnership with **American Education Defenders, Inc.**
AmericanEducationDefenders.org
paul@americaneducationdefenders.org

First Edition
Stand For Something
Volume 1 of the ***Bold Defenders*** Series in 3 Volumes
ISBN: 979-8-9926879-6-5
Library of Congress Control Number: 2025909384

Cover by Imesh and interior layout by the Author

This book is a work of creative nonfiction. While the character traits, values, and references are based on current and historical figures, commentary on legacies is dramatized for educational and inspirational purposes.

The sixteen values demonstrated in this book are introduced earlier in the **S**tand For Something: A Values Coloring Book For Kids, for younger readers, ages 7-12.

Praise for Stand For Something

"A very thought-provoking book that shows the timeless and unchanging nature of truth and good character. My teenager read it, and said that he can see the truth of it in the world around us today. Recommend!"
—Lynn Crandall, author of The Science of Homeschooling

"The book provides actionable tools, including exercises for parents to model resilience, spark discussions on identity, and empower teens to stand firm against peer pressure and ethical dilemmas. Through storytelling, subtle biblical undertones, and reflective prompts, Hemphill transforms potential victims of cultural chaos into proactive defenders of principle. His empowering tone frames character building as a bold, countercultural act that fosters lasting purpose and influence."
—Dr Jeffrey Horelick, research scientist and social media commentator

"Hemphill's insights, honed through years of experience, including service to our country, cuts through the noise to address a critical issue: the rise of nihilism among our youth, where meaning is scarce, and truth-seeking is overshadowed by cynicism. His book offers a compelling antidote, blending practical strategies with a heartfelt vision for nurturing virtues like integrity, resilience, wisdom, and purpose."
—Dr Eric Snyder, former Head of School, Norman, OK

"This book answers the call for calm waters in our troubled times and should be highly recommended inspirational reading for our youth. Author Paul Hemphill is a one-of-a-kind thought leader who is relentless in his pursuit of truth, justice and right reading."
—Judy Julin, Founder, CEO of WOWLearningLab

"For Christians, his message resonates deeply: faith is not passive, but active. Hemphill challenges readers to embrace values that reflect Christ's example—standing firm in truth, even when it costs us. His words remind us that discipleship

requires resolve, and that our witness is strongest when we live with clarity and conviction."
—*Stephen J. Smith, author of Social Media: Your Child's Digital Tattoo*

"This book should be in the hands of all parents and teachers! It's so practical and the real life experiences make the concepts/ topics very relatable even for younger children. I use this book with large groups of various ages at Reading Boot Camp. I use it as a resource. I have kids read straight from the book and sometimes I read a page to them. You can use it in so many ways and it's not on a screen! The scriptures that Paul adds really give each topic a punch of goodness!"
—*Kathy Alfke-Simpson, Head of Hillcrest Reading Boot Camp, Clinton, IN*

STAND FOR SOMETHING

A Guide to Character Formation
in a Culture That's Lost Its Way.

Paul Lloyd Hemphill

BOLD DEFENDERS SERIES
LINKED BY VALUES.
DEFINED BY CHARACTER.

Dedication

To my pre-teen grandchildren: Lyla, Anya, and Mason,
whose hearts are still unshaped by the noise,
whose eyes still see the world with wonder,
and whose innocence signals what's worth protecting.

May this book be a quiet guide for the days ahead
when choices get harder, voices get louder,
and standing for what's right feels lonely.

I wrote this for you
so you'll always remember that
truth is worth finding,
character is worth building,
and you are never alone when
you choose to stand.

Also by Paul Lloyd Hemphill

BOOKS
Gettysburg Lessons In The Digital Age
Why You're Already A Leader
Max Your Leadership!
Laughing With Leaders
Inspiration For Teens
Inspiration For Skeptics
Hair Force One
You're Awesome!
Planning For College
How To Play The College Game

Back Better Series
Bake Back Better
Bite Back Better
Bond Back Better

Bold Defenders Series
Stand For Something
America's Bold 52
Profiles In Character

and

Funnies of the Presidents (ChatGPT)
Surviving Teen Chaos (ChatGPT)
Watching Paint Dry (ChatGPT)

VIDEOS
America's 52 Stories

Table of Contents

Why I Couldn't Stay Silent 11
The Role of Wisdom 13
Introduction: Why This Book Matters 14

The Lie of "Just Be Yourself" 18
The Power of Truth 21
The Struggle for Authenticity 24
The Courage to Speak Up 27
The Strength of Character 31
The Importance of Boundaries 33
The Power of Saying "No" 37
The Power of Saying "Yes" 39
The Risk of Staying Silent 41
The Trap of Needing Approval 44
Standing When You Feel Alone 47
When Truth Isn't Popular 51
Choosing Conviction Over Comfort 54
When They Say, "That's Just Your Truth 57
"Don't Judge Me" — What Judgment Really Means 60
When Being "Nice" Isn't Enough 63
Standing Alone Without Feeling Alone 66
Strength Isn't Always Loud 69
What You Laugh At, You Learn From 72
The World's Approval Isn't Worth Your Soul 75
Courage Isn't Loud, But It's Real 78
You Weren't Made To Fit In 81
Don't Confuse Freedom With Chaos 84
Truth Isn't Trendy, And That's The Point 87
Being Offended Doesn't Make You Right 90
Conviction Isn't Hate 93
You Don't Need Everyone To Like You 96
Don't Trade Clarity For Acceptance 99

Courage Isn't Loud Either 101
You're Not Who They Say You Are 103
Opposition Doesn't Mean You're Wrong 105
You Can Be Bold Without Being Loud 107
You Don't Create Truth, You Align With It 109
You're Not The Only One 112
The Little Moments Count Most 115
Being Liked Is Overrated 118
Say The Hard Thing Anyway 122
The Culture You're Built To Stand In 125
Don't Just Stand There, Stand For Something 128

Graphic — What's The Purpose Of Values? 131
How To Discover What You Stand For 132
To Help You Discover Your Values 137
The 7-Day Stand-For-Something Challenge 139
The 16 Values: Historical and Biblical Roots 140
Bibliography 142
Appendix: For Homeschool Families and Church Leaders 147
About The Author 153

Why I Couldn't Stay Silent

I didn't plan to write this book.

But silence started to feel like surrender.

I looked around and saw teens being pulled in every direction—by influencers, trends, groupthink, and fear. I saw families unsure of how to guide their kids through it all without sounding either outdated or overwhelmed.

I saw a culture that calls lies "love," confusion "courage," and silence "wisdom." And I realized that if I stay quiet, I'm part of the problem.

So I wrote.

I wrote because too many young people are standing in storms without anchors.
I wrote because *character still matters*—even when culture pretends it doesn't.
And I wrote because **truth doesn't bend just because culture does.**

Some may wonder why I speak about Jesus in a book about standing strong in today's culture.
The truth is, I tried staying silent for a while. But the deeper I looked—at what makes people strong, what keeps families together, what gives young people a spine in a world full of pressure—the more I saw that it all points back to something deeper than opinion.
It points to truth.

I grew up Catholic. An altar boy for ten years. A soldier in Vietnam for thirteen months. I saw war up close, its madness and its toll. While coordinating the daily schedules of twenty chaplains, I expected to find faith alive. Instead, I found ambition in uniform: men chasing rank and medals, not the souls they were sent to serve. That revelation wounded my faith more deeply than combat ever could. Years later, when two members of my wife's family were abused by priests, the damage was nearly complete, not to my belief in God, but to my trust in those who claimed to speak for Him.

That was enough to make me walk away from the oldest institution on earth that protected the innocent, but was now protecting its image.

That's why I couldn't stay silent.

Then I rediscovered John Adams who wrote:

"Our Constitution was made only for a moral and religious people. It is wholly inadequate to the government of any other."

Adams was a realist sending us a warning: **Freedom falls apart when character disappears.**

And for Adams, *character was built on the teachings of Jesus of Nazareth.* So no, I'm not here to force you to swallow faith, but to help you discover its logic, its impact, and its proof.

Because if we want to raise teens who can stand for something, they'll need more than slogans and opinions.
They'll need **truth that doesn't move when the crowd does**.

If you've made it this far, then something in you refuses to drift. You're not here to float, you're here to **fight for what's true**.

So dig in. Speak up. And stand for something that won't crack under pressure.

Want to find out what you stand for—right now? Skip ahead to page 132 for a quick tool that helps you discover the values guiding your life today.

The Role Of Wisdom

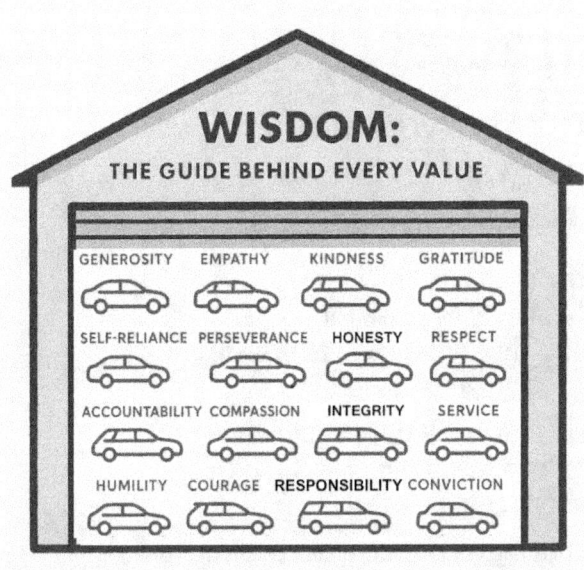

"Wisdom is knowing why things happen, not just that they do."
— Based on the teachings of Aristotle

Aristotle once said that wisdom isn't just knowledge, it's the ability to apply knowledge toward what is good. In this book, we didn't write a separate chapter on wisdom because we believe it shows up in all of them. Each of these values, such as generosity, courage, conviction, requires wisdom to know when, how, and how much to apply it.

That's why we say wisdom is like the garage that holds these 16 powerful vehicles. But it's more than storage. It's the light that flips on when the door lifts. It's the quiet voice that says, "Take courage today, leave pride parked." Wisdom doesn't just hold your values, it teaches you how to drive them.

What Is Character?

Character is a commitment to a set of values that never change.

That's why numbers and letters are called characters because they don't shift. They don't bend to pressure. They don't change with opinion.

In a world that constantly redefines what's right, real character stays fixed. It's not about being perfect.

It's about being anchored to something that doesn't move, especially when everything else does.

Discover what your values are starting on page **127**.

Introduction – Why This Book Matters

Culture isn't just changing, it's unraveling.
Every generation faces pressure. But this one? It's being crushed under the weight of confusion.
Identity, truth, morality, and even purpose, once taken for granted, are now up for debate.
Everything is fluid. Everything is optional. Everything is... negotiable.

So what's left to stand on?

The Struggle to Stand Firm
Sometimes, standing firm in your beliefs feels impossible.
It feels like you'll lose friends or face rejection.
It might make you uncomfortable, misunderstood, or even mocked.

But here's the thing:
Standing firm is always worth the risk.
It may be hard in the moment, but it will lead you to a place of strength and clarity in the long run.

Real Teen Example: Sarah from Denver, CO
Sarah felt overwhelmed by the pressure to fit in and be like everyone else. She was caught in a constant cycle of comparison, trying to meet others' expectations. But when Sarah stopped trying to please everyone and focused on her own beliefs and values, she discovered a new kind of peace —living authentically. Sarah's choice to embrace who she

truly was, rather than conforming, gave her the stability and strength she had been searching for in a world full of confusion.

Why Standing Firm Builds Strength
Standing firm takes courage.
It takes courage to go against the flow when everyone else is conforming.
It takes courage to speak up when the truth isn't popular.
It takes courage to live your values even when no one else seems to.

But every time you choose to stand firm, you build **character**.
You strengthen your inner core.
And you teach others to respect you, not just when it's easy, but when it's hard.

Bold Defender: Michael from San Diego, CA
Michael tried to live by the world's expectations, always pushing himself to be "perfect." He thought that being perfect would lead him to acceptance and fulfillment. But after struggling with the pressure to meet everyone else's standards, he made a powerful shift. He started embracing his core values and focusing on being true to himself, not what others expected. This choice allowed his relationships to deepen and his confidence to grow, as he realized that true peace comes from staying true to your values, not living for others.

Standing Firm Isn't Just About Words, It's About Living The Truth
Standing firm isn't just about **what you say**; it's about **how you live**.
You can say the right things, but it doesn't matter if your actions don't match.

Living with integrity means aligning your words with your actions every single day.

True strength isn't just about speaking up, it's about being the same person on the outside as you are on the inside.

The Cost of Living a Lie
Living a lie may seem easier, but it takes more effort than standing in the truth.
A lie weighs on you, it eats away at your peace, and it forces you to hide who you really are.

But standing firm in truth?
Standing firm makes life lighter.
It allows you to live authentically, without the weight of pretending or hiding.

Truth For Teens
The world will tell you it's easier to hide, to lie, or to cover up.
But standing firm in the truth will always lead to strength.

Standing firm makes you free, authentic, and powerful.

Here are 2 Questions for Parents, Mentors, and Teens to discuss after each chapter:

1. What's the main message of this chapter, and how does it apply to my life right now?
2. Is there a choice or situation this week where I could live this out more boldly?

Chapter 1 – The Lie of "Just Be Yourself"

Sounds harmless, right?

"Just be yourself."
It's on T-shirts. Posters. TikToks.
It's said by celebrities, teachers, even pastors.

But here's the truth:
That advice can be one of the most dangerous things you believe.

Why? Because It Leaves Out the Most Important Question:

Which self?

The one that wants to scroll all night?
The one that gets jealous for no reason?
The one that lashes out, hides, quits, or doubts?

Let's be honest: sometimes the *"self"* we are isn't the self we're proud of.

So what happens when someone tells you, "Just be yourself," and the version of yourself you're living isn't strong, healthy, or wise?

You stay stuck.
And worse, you start to believe that staying stuck is *authentic*.

You're Not a Finished Product

You're not supposed to be "yourself."
You're supposed to **grow**.
Truth isn't about accepting everything you feel.
It's about **aligning who you are with who you were made to become**.

God didn't design you to stay as you are.
He designed you to be transformed.

Growth Takes Work

The real challenge isn't being yourself.
It's becoming who you're called to be.

That takes:

- Humility
- Discipline
- Character
- And truth that cuts through the fluff

The world wants you to stay comfortable.
God wants you to grow stronger.

Big difference.

Real Identity Isn't Found, It's Built

When you follow Jesus, you don't lose your identity.
You find the version that was buried under sin, fear, and noise.

It's not about becoming someone fake.
It's about becoming someone **others look up to**.

So don't settle for the version of you that culture claps for.
Become the version God designed you to become.

Your Takeaways
Don't "be yourself."
Be the self that grows. The self that learns. The self that leads.

You weren't made to stay the same.
You were made to stand out and rise up, which brings us to…

…John Adams, who didn't think "be yourself" was good advice. He knew that people aren't perfect, and if you just follow your feelings, you'll end up focused on yourself instead of what's right. His answer was simple but powerful: picture the kind of person you want to be and work every day to become that person.

Better still, find someone you admire, someone who lives with honesty, courage, and faith, and learn from him or her. By imitating what's good in others, you start to shape that same goodness in yourself.

Adams believed that true strength and virtue came from the teachings of Jesus, especially the Sermon on the Mount, which he saw as a guide for living with humility, discipline, and purpose.

He also knew that freedom could only last if both citizens and their leaders lived by those same values.

That's what this book is all about: learning how to build the kind of strength and character that make your life meaningful and your country strong.

Chapter 2 – The Power of Truth

Truth isn't always easy to find.
In a world filled with opinions, filters, likes, and noise, it's easy to mistake popularity for reality.
But here's the thing:
Truth doesn't change.

Even when the world shifts, even when people lie, even when trends move, truth stays the same.

You don't get to decide truth.
You get to **discover it.**

The Challenge of Living in Truth

Telling the truth is one thing.
Living the truth, that's harder.
It means standing for something even when you're the only one standing.
It means saying what's right, even when it's not what people want to hear.
It means refusing to pretend.

Truth is the foundation that builds strong character.
It grounds your decisions, guides your relationships, and clears the fog when everything else feels uncertain.

Real Teen Example: Maya from Charlotte, NC
Maya always thought she had to agree with everyone to be liked. She'd nod along, laugh at jokes she didn't find funny, and go along with things she didn't believe in. One day, a rumor started about a classmate she knew wasn't true.

Everyone else went quiet, but Maya spoke up. She told the truth, even though it made things awkward. In the days that followed, more people came to respect her, not for agreeing with them, but for being brave enough to stand apart. That one moment taught her that truth has power, and it also has weight. But it was worth carrying.

Why Truth is Stronger Than Image
We live in a world that worships appearances.
We're told to polish, perform, and pretend.
But the most magnetic people in the world aren't the most polished.
They're the most **real**.

And real people are anchored in truth.
They don't try to be everything to everyone.
They let their yes be yes, their no be no, and their life match their words.

Bold Defender: Joe Rogan - Cultural Influencer
You wouldn't expect a guy like Joe Rogan, a comedian, podcaster, and voice of one of the biggest shows in the world, to start talking about Jesus. But he did. In a conversation about science and belief, he said, "People will be incredulous about the resurrection of Jesus Christ, but yet they're convinced that the entire universe was smaller than the head of a pin... and became everything?" Then he said something even more surprising: **"I'm sticking with Jesus on that one. Jesus makes more sense."** And he didn't stop there. **"We need Jesus. For real... now's a good time."** That's coming from a guy with millions of followers who's never been known for quoting Scripture. But even he sees it: **truth cuts through the noise.** That kind of honesty stands out, not because it's loud, but because it's real.

Truth Isn't Always Loud, But It's Always Clear
You don't have to shout to live the truth.
You just have to stop pretending.
The world doesn't need more noise. It needs more clarity.
And you can be a source of that.

When people know they can trust you, really trust you, your words carry weight.
Not because you're perfect.
But because you're **honest**.

Because when you live the truth, you're not just making a point, you're building your character.

Truth is what's right.
Character is the courage to live like it matters.

Truth doesn't change.
Character is what grows when you keep choosing that truth even when it's hard, unpopular, or inconvenient.

Truth and character go hand in hand.
Truth is what's real even when people deny it, ignore it, or try to twist it.
Character is what you build when you choose to live by that truth.
You can't have strong character without a strong foundation.
And that foundation is truth—steady, solid, and unchanging.

"Then you will know the truth, and the truth will set you free." — *John 8:32*

Chapter 3 – The Struggle for Authenticity

Authenticity sounds simple.
Be real. Be you.
But in a world that rewards image, filters, and surface-level success, authenticity takes guts.

The truth is, it's easier to wear a mask than to live without one.
Easier to blend in than to stand out.
Easier to perform than to be seen.

But if you want to live with real confidence, you'll need to stop performing and start showing up.

Why It's Hard to Be Real

We're surrounded by expectations.
You're supposed to look a certain way, act a certain way, post the right stuff, say the right things.
And somewhere in all of that… you disappear.

You begin to wonder if your real self is enough.
So you hide it.
You create a version of you that others will accept even if it isn't true.

Real Teen Example: Brielle from Sacramento, CA
Brielle was the funny one. Always smiling, always making jokes, always keeping the energy light. But underneath, she was struggling. She hated feeling fake but didn't think

anyone would like the quiet, serious version of her. One day, she opened up during a class presentation about anxiety, and her classmates didn't mock her. They leaned in. A few even thanked her afterward for being honest. That moment changed everything. She realized the version of herself she thought no one would accept was the one people connected with the most.

Why Authenticity Builds Strength

Being real doesn't mean being perfect.
It means being consistent.
When you stop changing who you are based on who's in the room, you start building trust with others and with yourself.

Authenticity builds resilience.
You don't have to keep track of who you're pretending to be.
You don't have to protect an image.
You just live.

And that freedom?
It's strength.

Bold Defender: Amir from Raleigh, NC
Amir always dressed, talked, and acted the way his friend group expected. But deep down, he hated how fake it felt. He loved writing and reading history, things his friends made fun of. Eventually, he started spending time with people who liked those same things. It was awkward at first, but it didn't take long to feel natural. His old friends faded. His real life began. Now, Amir says the best thing he ever did was "stop trying to impress and start trying to live."

What Authenticity Is And What It Isn't

Authenticity isn't about oversharing.
It's not about being loud or dramatic.
It's not about being "different" just to get attention.

It's about alignment.
Your values match your voice.
Your beliefs match your behavior.
Your identity doesn't change just to avoid judgment.

Authenticity is quiet power.
The kind that doesn't need applause to know it's doing the right thing.

Your Takeaways
It's tempting to hide.
To shape-shift into whoever people want you to be.

But that version of you? It's a shell.
And it can crack at any moment.

When you live authentically, you build a life that can't be shaken because it's not built on lies.

Be consistent. Be real. Be free.

The real you is the strongest version there is.

Chapter 4 – The Courage to Speak Up

Sometimes, staying quiet feels safer.
It's easier to nod along.
Easier to keep the peace.
Easier to avoid the drama.

But silence can cost more than words ever will.
Especially when you're watching something wrong happen right in front of you.

Speaking up takes courage because it almost always comes with a risk.
But staying silent comes with one too: regret.

Why We Stay Silent

We don't want to offend anyone.
We don't want to stand out.
We don't want to lose friends or be labeled "dramatic" or "difficult."

So we laugh at what we don't agree with.
We go along with what we know is wrong.
And we swallow our words when we were born to speak.

Real Teen Example: Tiana from Baltimore, MD
Tiana was in a group chat with her classmates when someone started making fun of another girl who wasn't in it. Everyone laughed. Tiana didn't. She sat there, watching the screen, heart pounding. Then she did something bold: she

messaged, "This isn't right. I'm out." She left the chat. Later, two classmates privately thanked her. And the teasing stopped. That one sentence? It took three seconds to type, but it changed the tone of the whole group and changed how Tiana saw her own voice.

*Courage without **wisdom** becomes recklessness.*

Why Speaking Up Builds Character

You don't have to shout.
You don't have to be loud.
You just have to be clear.

When you speak up for what's right, you don't just protect others, you protect your own integrity.

Every time you use your voice, you become stronger.
You show others that silence doesn't always win.
And you lead by example even if no one claps for it.

Bold Defender: Xavier from Wichita, KS

Xavier used to think staying quiet made him wise. He avoided conflict at all costs even when he saw people getting mistreated. But after witnessing a teacher being mocked by students over and over, something in him changed. One day, he calmly said in front of the whole class, "You don't have to like every teacher. But you don't have to be cruel either." It got quiet. No one responded. But after that, the jokes stopped. Xavier didn't speak again that day, but he didn't need to. His courage had already done its work.

What Speaking Up Really Means

Speaking up isn't just about defending others.
Sometimes, it's about defending **truth**.

Or defending **yourself**.
It's about not letting fear make you smaller.

It means setting boundaries.
Saying no.
Naming what's wrong.
And doing it without becoming harsh, rude, or arrogant.

Courage doesn't come from volume.
It comes from conviction.

Wisdom turns courage into conviction, not chaos.

Your Takeaways
The world doesn't need more noise.
It needs more clarity.

And sometimes that clarity comes through one voice that refuses to stay silent.

You don't need a crowd behind you to speak the truth.
You just need a spine.
A steady voice.
And a belief that truth is worth defending.

When you speak up with courage, you don't just change the moment, you change the atmosphere.

Fake tolerance says: *"Lie to keep the peace."*
Real courage says: *"Tell the truth with love, not fear."*

You can be kind.
You can be respectful.
But you cannot give away your convictions just to fit in.

Character includes the courage to stay kind without staying silent.

"Our lives begin to end the day we become silent about things that matter."
　　　　　　　　　　— *Martin Luther King, Jr*

Chapter 5 - The Strength of Character

In a world full of noise, attention is cheap.
Loud gets noticed.
Viral gets rewarded.
But none of that lasts.

What lasts is character.
Character doesn't always shine in the spotlight.
But it always shows up when it matters.

Why Character Still Matters

Character isn't just about doing the right thing.
It's about doing it when no one's watching.
It's about being the same person in private that you pretend to be in public.

Character is a commitment to a set of values that never change. That commitment isn't glamorous.
It won't always make you popular.
But it will make you solid.

Real Teen Example — Simone from Tulsa, OK
Simone was elected class secretary mostly because she was friendly and well-liked. But halfway through the year, she found out the president was taking credit for things she and others had done. Everyone told her to let it go, it would just cause drama. But Simone knew it wasn't right. In the next meeting, she calmly and respectfully laid out what had really happened. It wasn't about revenge, it was about truth. That moment made her more respected than any popularity vote ever could.

What Character Actually Looks Like
Character isn't flashy.

It's not about being a "good kid" or having a clean image.
It's deeper than that.

It's **consistency**.
It's showing up even when it's boring.
It's doing the hard thing even when no one gives you credit.
It's staying grounded when the world is pulling you in every direction.

It's being **committed to a set of values that never change**.

Bold Defender — Jordan from Portland, ME
Jordan's parents didn't push him to go to church or follow any particular path. He had a lot of freedom and a lot of chances to mess around. But somewhere along the way, Jordan decided he wanted to live differently. He started reading leadership books, showing up early to work, and helping classmates who needed it. No one told him to. Most people didn't even notice. But it changed his life and eventually caught the attention of a coach who offered him a scholarship for his quiet, steady leadership. Character opened doors that charisma never could.

Why Character Will Always Outlast Cool

Trends come and go.
Reputations rise and fall.
But character? It builds. It lasts.

Character earns trust.
It gives you influence without having to shout.
It lets people know that when everything else shakes, you don't.

Because you're not just performing.
You're built differently.

Your Takeaways
Your personality might open doors.
But it's your character that keeps them open.

The world will push you to be bold, loud, likable, or funny.
But the world doesn't need more noise.
It needs more people who are consistent, real, and solid.

Committed to a set of values, like what you see starting on page 128.

Be the one who's committed.
Be the one who doesn't fold under pressure.
Be the one people can trust.

Character is strength, and it never goes out of style.

What Is Character?

Character is a commitment to a set of values that never change.

That's why numbers and letters are called characters—because they don't shift. They don't bend to pressure. They don't change with opinion.

In a world that constantly redefines what's right, real character stays fixed. It's not about being perfect.

It's about being anchored to something that doesn't move—especially when everything else does.

"A good man brings good things out of the good stored up in his heart... for the mouth speaks what the heart is full of."
— *Luke 6:45*

Chapter 6 – The Importance of Boundaries

It's easy to feel like the "nice" thing to do is say yes to everything.
Be chill.
Be agreeable.
Be flexible.

But saying yes to everything eventually means saying no to yourself.

Boundaries aren't about pushing people away.
They're about protecting what matters most.

Why We Avoid Setting Boundaries

We don't want to disappoint anyone.
We're afraid of being misunderstood.
We think we'll seem selfish or mean.

So we stay in conversations that drain us.
We laugh at jokes that make us uncomfortable.
We give time, energy, and attention to things that leave us empty.

Real Teen Example — Ava from Nashville, TN

Ava was the friend everyone counted on. Always available. Always listening. Always giving. But over time, she realized she was saying yes to so many people that she had no time to recharge. She felt used and invisible. One day, she decided to start small: she turned off her phone one weekend and told her friends she needed rest. To her surprise, no one got mad. In fact, a few of them admitted they wished they could do the same. That weekend became the start of her learning how to say "no" without guilt and "yes" to what truly mattered.

*Service without **wisdom** becomes self-sacrifice that helps no one.*

Why Boundaries Build Respect

The people who matter will respect your boundaries.
The people who don't? They were never safe to begin with.

Boundaries teach others how to treat you.
They make it clear:
This is what I allow.
This is what I don't.
This is how I expect to be respected.

And every time you enforce a boundary, you reinforce your worth.

Bold Defender — Elijah from Jacksonville, FL

Elijah found himself surrounded by a group that constantly mocked others. At first, he played along just to belong. But it didn't sit right with him. One day, after yet another cruel joke, he quietly said, "That's not cool, man," and walked away. The group was stunned. A couple of them laughed. But one person followed him after and said, "Thanks. I wanted to say something too." Elijah didn't just protect his peace, he gave someone else the courage to do the same.

What Boundaries Are and What They Aren't

Boundaries aren't walls.
They're filters.
They help you let the right people in and keep the wrong behavior out.

Boundaries aren't about control.
They're about clarity.
You're not trying to dominate anyone.
You're simply drawing lines that protect your peace, your time, and your values

Your Takeaways
Setting boundaries doesn't make you selfish.
It makes you wise.

When you learn to say no to what drains you,
You make space to say yes to what grows you.

You don't owe unlimited access to anyone.
You owe your best self the space to thrive.

Speak clearly.
Stand kindly.
Hold the line.

Your peace is worth protecting.

"The first and greatest victory is to conquer yourself."
                    Plato (Ancient Greek philosopher)

Chapter 7 – The Power of Saying "No"

We live in a world that constantly says "more."
More activities.
More likes.
More opportunities.
More yes.

But here's the truth:
Saying yes to everything will eventually break you.

Sometimes the strongest thing you can do is say **no**.

Why Saying No Feels Wrong

You don't want to seem rude.
You don't want to miss out.
You don't want people to think you're weak, scared, or judgmental.

So you go along with things that don't feel right.
You say yes to commitments that exhaust you.
You give energy to people who drain you.

But every "yes" to the wrong thing is a "no" to something better.

Real Teen Example: Natalie from Phoenix, AZ

Natalie got invited to every hangout. She was friendly, always down for fun, and never wanted to be left out. But the more she said yes, the less time she had for her goals, especially the writing project she kept putting off. One night, she made a tough decision: she turned down a party to stay home and finish her short story. It wasn't a glamorous move, but it felt right. Two weeks later, she submitted the piece to a national teen contest—and won second place. That one "no" created space for a much bigger "yes."

*Self-reliance is strength, but **wisdom** knows when to say no.*

What You Say "No" To Shapes Your Life

No to peer pressure.
No to distractions.
No to things that feel fake, forced, or off-track.

Every no is a boundary.
And boundaries shape identity.
They define who you are **not** so you can become who you **are**.

Bold Defender: Isaiah from Tampa, FL
Isaiah played varsity sports, kept good grades, and had big college plans. But one night, his friends invited him to a party that he knew could spiral. It wasn't just about rules, it was about character. He politely declined. His friends rolled their eyes and called him boring. But the next day, three people got suspended for what happened at that party. Isaiah wasn't relieved because he "dodged trouble," he was proud because he made a decision based on who he wanted to be, not who others expected him to be.

Saying No Isn't About Fear. It's About Focus.

You don't say no because you're scared.
You say no because you're committed.
You say no because you've decided who you are and who you're not.

Saying no means taking ownership of your path.
It means refusing to let other people steer your life.

It means choosing long-term purpose over short-term approval.

Your Takeaways
Not every opportunity is worth your time.
Not every invitation is a door you should walk through.
Say no when something feels wrong.
Say no when it distracts you from your values.
Say no when you know deep down: this isn't who I want to be.

Saying no doesn't make you weak.
It makes you wise.

Chapter 8 – The Power of Saying "Yes"

We talk a lot about saying **no** to pressure, distractions, and lies.
But sometimes the **boldest move** you can make is saying **yes**.

Yes to purpose.
Yes to growth.
Yes to something that stretches you beyond what's comfortable.

Because while saying no builds strength, saying yes—at the right time—**builds direction**.

Why It's Hard to Say Yes

Saying yes means stepping into the unknown.
It means responsibility.
It means challenge.
It means risk.

Most people would rather coast.
Take the easy class.
Join the easy crowd.
Choose the path that asks the least.

But if you always choose easy, you'll never choose meaningful.

Real Teen Example: Jordan from Minneapolis, MN
Jordan was invited to speak at his school's leadership summit. He almost said no. Public speaking terrified him. But something inside told him to say yes even if his voice shook. He spent two weeks preparing, almost backed out the night before, and still said yes. And that yes changed everything. After his talk, two classmates told him they saw

themselves in his story. Jordan didn't just overcome fear, he discovered he had something to say. That one yes unlocked a new confidence and direction he hadn't felt before.

*Conviction means holding firm, but **wisdom** means knowing when to lean in.*

What Saying Yes Unlocks

Saying yes means leaning into the opportunity instead of running from it. It means choosing challenge over comfort. It means letting your life get bigger than fear.

You will not grow without discomfort.
You will not lead without risk. You will not change the world from the sidelines.

Saying yes is what gets you in the game.

Bold Defender: Kayla from Boise, ID
Kayla got a chance to mentor younger girls through her youth group. She almost laughed it off; she didn't think she was qualified. But her leader said, "Just be honest, and show up." So she said yes. Over the next three months, she found herself answering questions, offering advice, and most of all, **listening**. By saying yes, she didn't just help others, she grew herself. Now, Kayla sees leadership not as something flashy, but as something built through small, steady yeses.

Kayla learned something powerful:
Listening isn't just a skill, it's a reflection of character. When you listen with patience and honesty, you're showing humility, respect, and strength. *These are real values.*

You're putting someone else first.
And that's what real character does.

You don't have to be the loudest to lead.
Sometimes, the most powerful thing you can do is show up, lean in, and truly listen.

When Yes Means Purpose

Saying yes doesn't mean saying yes to everything.
It means saying yes to the **right things,** things that grow you, stretch you, and align with your values.

Your time is limited.
So your yes has power.
Make it count.

Say yes to the uncomfortable conversation.
Say yes to the better choice.
Say yes to the opportunity that scares you *in a good way.*

Every meaningful life is built on a series of intentional, courageous yeses.

It's saying yes to your set of values.

Your Takeaways
The world is full of easy outs and low expectations.
But your future doesn't need easy.
It needs **intentional.**
It needs **strong.**
It needs **purpose-driven.**
It needs **values-commitment.**

Your yes can be small, but powerful.
Every time you choose purpose over comfort, you rise.

So don't waste your yes.
Aim it at something that matters.

Chapter 9 – The Risk of Staying Silent

There's a moment you'll face.
A conversation. A classroom. A group of friends.
Something's said that isn't right.
And you feel it deep in your gut.

You want to speak.
But you freeze.

And just like that, the moment passes.
The truth goes unspoken.
And silence wins again.

Why Silence Feels Safer

It's safer not to interrupt.
It's easier to laugh along.
It feels smarter to blend in than to call something out.

But every time you stay silent when you were made to speak, a piece of your confidence slips away.
You wonder later why you didn't say something.
And you promise next time, you will.

Real Teen Example: Kayla from Indianapolis, IN
Kayla overheard a student spreading a rumor about someone she barely knew. At first, she said nothing. But the next day, that rumor had spread, and the girl it was about was in tears. Kayla couldn't shake the guilt. She went back to the source, told the truth, and cleared things up. It didn't make her the hero, but it did make her real. That experience showed her that silence doesn't protect anyone. Sometimes, it allows harm to keep spreading.

*Empathy without **wisdom** can turn silence into surrender.*

Why Speaking Up Isn't About Volume

You don't have to be loud.
You don't have to confront people aggressively.
You just have to be willing to say, "That's not right,"
Or even, "I'm not okay with this."

Truth has power even when spoken softly.

Bold Defender: Ethan from Salt Lake City, UT
Ethan was in a friend group that often made offhand jokes about others, nothing too cruel, but always cutting. He'd laugh nervously, trying to fit in. Until one day, someone turned the joke on him. It stung. Badly. He realized he had been going along with something that didn't match his values. That night, he sent a simple message to the group: "Hey, I'm stepping back from these convos. It's been weighing on me." No argument. No drama. Just clarity. A few others followed. It only took one honest voice to change the room.

The Cost of Silence

Silence isn't always neutral.
Sometimes it's a slow erosion of your identity.
It chips away at your sense of courage.
At your alignment with truth.
At your self-respect.

If you stay silent too long,
You'll forget what your voice sounds like.

But every time you speak up,
You take a step closer to becoming who you really are.

Your Takeaways
The world doesn't need more noise.
It needs more voices that speak with purpose.
Voices that demonstrate a commitment to values.

If something's wrong, don't stay quiet.
If something matters, say so.
If truth is being ignored, bring it back into the light.

Your voice doesn't have to be perfect.
It just has to be **used**.

Speak when it's hard.
And watch your strength grow.

Chapter 10 – The Trap of Needing Approval

We all want to be liked.
To be seen.
To be chosen.

But when **approval becomes the goal**, it becomes a trap.
You start saying what people want to hear.
Doing what they want you to do.
Becoming who they want you to be.

And in the process, you lose something much bigger: **yourself**.

Why Approval Feels Addictive

Every like. Every compliment.
Every laugh.
It feels good.
But it's never enough.

You crave more.
So you perform. You please. You pretend.
You hold back your voice.
You tone down your convictions.
You build your life on feedback.
And call it confidence.

Real Teen Example: Mia from San Diego, CA
Mia loved performing: drama club, speeches, anything on stage. But offstage, she was completely different. She said yes to every favor. Smiled through every insult. Laughed at jokes that hurt. Why? Because she didn't want to lose anyone's approval. One day, her drama teacher pulled her

aside and asked, "Do you even know who you are when you're

you're not performing?" That question shook her. Slowly, she started saying no when she needed to. And the crazy part? The people who actually cared about her respected her more for it.

Compassion without **wisdom** *loses its voice.*

What You Lose by Needing Everyone to Like You

You lose your boundaries.
You lose your voice.
You lose your ability to make choices based on **truth** because you're too busy chasing reactions.

The more you need everyone's approval,
the more you become a reflection of what they want
instead of who you really are.

Bold Defender: Marcus from Atlanta, GA
Marcus was known for being "chill." Always easygoing. Always agreeable. But deep down, he hated how little people actually knew him. He had strong beliefs, deep questions, big goals, but none of it ever came out. He was afraid it might make him uncool. Eventually, he decided to stop hiding. He started posting real thoughts, speaking up in class, and hanging out with people who actually saw him. It was awkward at first, but freeing. And for the first time, he didn't just feel liked. He felt known.

Approval Isn't the Goal, Integrity Is

You don't have to be rude.
You don't have to be cold.
You just have to stop pretending.

When you act out of approval addiction, you become a character
instead of building character.

Real confidence isn't about being liked.
It's about being **aligned**
with your values, your convictions, and your truth.

Your Takeaways
You weren't made to be liked by everyone.
You were made to be **true**.

Approval fades.
Trends change.
Crowds move on.

But integrity?
That lasts.
Because it's a value that never changes.

Don't trade who you are for who they want.
Your voice is too valuable.
And your life is too important to be lived by committee.

"Character is like a tree and reputation like its shadow. The shadow is what we think of it; the tree is the real thing."
— *Abraham Lincoln*

Chapter 11 – Standing When You Feel Alone

Sometimes the hardest thing isn't knowing what's right.
It's choosing to do it **alone**.

When the crowd goes one way, and you feel like the only one going another,
Your legs shake.
Your voice gets quiet.
And you wonder, *Why bother?*

But here's what you need to know:
Courage doesn't come from company.
It comes from conviction.

Why Loneliness Can Feel Louder Than Truth

We were made to belong.
So when we stand for something others don't understand,
that silence can feel like rejection.

And rejection?

It's loud.
It tells you to back down. To sit down. To shut up.
Even if your heart says otherwise.

Real Teen Example: Nora from Charleston, SC
Nora was the only one in her friend group who still believed in saving sex for marriage. At first, she laughed it off when people teased her. But then came the rumors. The jokes. The distance. It stung. She considered pretending to believe differently just to fit back in. Instead, she had one honest

conversation with a classmate who respected her decision and unexpectedly gained a new friendship grounded in respect, not performance. It reminded her that standing alone doesn't always mean staying alone.

Wisdom *reminds us that isolation isn't always a signal to retreat sometimes, it's proof you're walking the harder, higher road.*

What Happens When You Choose to Stand Anyway

You get clearer.
Stronger.
Quieter, but more confident.
You realize that sometimes **you are the example** someone else is waiting for.

And while it may cost you in the moment,
It builds something unshakable in the long run.

Bold Defender: Marcus from Bozeman, MT
Marcus was in a school club where most conversations drifted toward cynicism and constant negativity. One day, after a particularly dark meeting, he raised his hand and said, "Can we talk about something good for once?" The room went silent. Someone snickered. But the next week, a few others came prepared with stories about people doing good things in the world. It didn't turn into a revival, but it shifted the tone. And Marcus realized he didn't need a crowd to change the atmosphere. He just needed the guts to start.

Alone Doesn't Mean Wrong

Feeling alone doesn't mean you're off-track.
It often means you're ahead.
It means you're listening to something deeper than approval.
You're anchored to truth, not swayed by opinion.

And that kind of character?
That's rare.
That's real.
That's powerful.

Your Takeaways
Standing alone might look weak from the outside.
But it's actually one of the boldest things you can do.

Don't fold for comfort.
Don't shrink for safety.
Don't pretend to blend in when you were made to stand out.

Courage isn't loud.
Sometimes, it's just **standing** when no one else will.

"Character cannot be developed in ease and quiet. Only through experience of trial and suffering can the soul be strengthened."
— *Helen Keller*

Chapter 12 – When Truth Isn't Popular

I once heard someone describe truth like this:
"I was seated in a crowded hall and I yelled, 'What is truth?' and then I ran out the back door, not wanting to hear the answer."

It stuck with me, not just for its honesty, but for what it says about us.
We like to ask big questions. We say we want truth, but only the kind that makes us feel good. Not the kind that changes us.

Because truth doesn't just comfort, it confronts. It tells us when we're wrong. And sometimes, we'd rather run than face it.

Real character doesn't flinch. It leans in.
Culture runs. You don't have to.

Wisdom *doesn't just seek comfort, it seeks what's real, even when the truth cuts against the grain.*

It's easy to assume truth is welcome. That if you speak honestly and respectfully, people will listen.
But in today's world, truth can make you a target.

Once, colleges were beacons. They chased truth. Tested it. Defended it.

Today, many have replaced that pursuit with something cheaper: opinion disguised as fact, ideology paraded as scholarship, and emotion treated as evidence.

Instead of shaping minds, some institutions now shape narratives, pushing students to conform, not question. To repeat, not reason.

They've become fountains of misinformation where feelings outweigh facts, and where standing for something real, like character or truth, is seen as outdated or even offensive.

But truth hasn't disappeared. It's buried under noise.
Your job, if you're bold enough, is to dig it up, brush it off, and stand for it anyway.

When you take a stand on what matters most, you might be mocked.
You might be canceled. But that doesn't make you wrong. It just means truth still makes people uncomfortable.

Why Popularity Can't Be Your Compass

Popularity feels good for a moment.
But it shifts like the wind. One day you're in. The next, you're invisible.

If you chase popularity, you'll compromise truth.
You'll water down conviction to avoid rejection.
You'll soften what's real to fit what's trendy.

And in the end, you'll lose the only thing that matters: your integrity.

Real Teen Example: Naomi from Jacksonville, FL
Naomi, a straight-A student, loved both science and faith. During a class discussion, she shared that her belief in God deepened her interest in biology. Some classmates laughed. For a moment, she wished she'd stayed quiet. But after class, a quiet student whispered, "Thank you. I believe that too." It reminded her: not all respect is loud, and not all mockery means you're wrong.

What Happens When You Speak Unpopular Truth

You might feel tension.
You might lose approval.
But you'll gain clarity.

And you'll sleep better at night knowing you didn't hide.
Truth isn't a trend. It's a foundation.

Bold Defender: Eli from New Haven, CT

During a debate on morality, Eli said some truths—like honesty and dignity—are universal. Some students called him narrow-minded. But his teacher nodded and said, "That's an important perspective, don't let go of it." Eli didn't win the room. But he walked out stronger. He spoke from conviction, not for applause.

Truth Doesn't Need Permission

Truth doesn't need a crowd.
It doesn't need a vote or a platform.
It just needs you to stand for it even when it costs you.

Because if you give up truth for popularity,
You'll always have to perform to keep your place.
But if you stand for truth, you can stand in peace.

Your Takeaways

Truth may not always trend.
But it will always matter.
Don't trade clarity for claps.
Don't trade peace for popularity.

Don't be afraid to be the one voice that speaks when others stay silent.

"Some truths don't need to be shouted—just carried."

Stand for truth because truth will
still be standing when the crowd has moved on.
And when you live the truth, you're not just making a point, you're building your character.

Chapter 13 – Choosing Conviction Over Comfort

Conviction is knowing what's right
and choosing to live it out, even when it's uncomfortable.

Comfort is easy. It's safe.
It keeps you liked.
It keeps you quiet.

But nothing meaningful is built in comfort.
Real growth happens when you **live what you believe even when it's hard.**

Why Comfort Can Quiet Your Convictions

When you're surrounded by people who disagree, it's tempting to go along.
You smile, nod, maybe even laugh just to keep the peace.

But afterward, something doesn't feel right.

Because deep down, you know you weren't true to yourself.
You didn't speak. You didn't walk away.
You chose comfort and sacrificed conviction.

Wisdom *asks, "What kind of person are you becoming?" especially when the easy road tempts you to forget what you believe.*

Real Teen Example: Grace from Cedar Rapids, IA

Grace was just 15 when a girl in her class said she was considering an abortion. Most students stayed silent. Some gave advice. Grace listened and then asked, "Do you want to talk to someone who's been through this before?" She connected her classmate with a mentor who had chosen life years earlier. That girl didn't get an abortion. They never became close friends. But months later, she messaged Grace:

"You're the only person who didn't treat me like a political issue. You saw me as a person."

Why Conviction Builds Confidence

Conviction gives you a spine.
It keeps you standing when the world tells you to sit down.
You won't fold under pressure, or trade your values for approval.

Bold Defender: Caleb from Des Moines, IA

Caleb was the only guy on his team who refused to vape. They teased him constantly. He started making excuses to skip out, avoiding the pressure. Then a teammate had a health scare and ended up in the ER.

Grace didn't win a crowd.
She didn't post about it.
She just stood quietly—for life,
for compassion, and for courage.
That's character.

Suddenly, Caleb's quiet stance looked like wisdom.
He didn't gloat. He didn't say, "I told you so."
He just stayed consistent.

Weeks later, two teammates asked him for help quitting.
Caleb wasn't the loudest voice, but he became the one they trusted when it mattered.

When Conviction Costs Something

You might get laughed at.
You might feel alone.

But here's what you gain:
Clarity.
Strength.
And the kind of confidence that comes from knowing you didn't back down when it counted.

Conviction might cost you something short-term,
but it builds a life you won't regret.

Your Takeaways

Conviction means doing what's right even when it costs you something.

Comfort feels good in the moment, but it won't build a life you're proud of.

You don't have to shout to stand strong, just be consistent.

When you stay true to what you believe, others will notice.

Don't trade your values for approval. Character lasts longer than popularity.

———

"If you look for truth, you may find comfort in the end; if you look for comfort you will not get either comfort or truth— only soft soap and wishful thinking to begin with."
— *C.S. Lewis*

Chapter 14: When They Say, "That's Just Your Truth"

You've probably heard it before: "Well, that's *your* truth." Or maybe: "What's true for you isn't necessarily true for me."

Sounds polite. Open-minded, even. But here's the problem: **truth doesn't change just because someone doesn't like it.** If truth were just based on feelings, opinions, or trends, we'd never agree on anything. Ever.

Imagine you're taking a math test and you write that 2 + 2 = 5. When your teacher marks it wrong, you say, "Well, that's *your* truth." That wouldn't fly, right? Because some things, like math, gravity, and moral truth, **aren't up for debate.**

The Culture of "Whatever"

Our culture pushes the idea that everyone creates their own truth. It sounds freeing at first until you realize it's a trap. If everything is "your truth," then nothing is *the* truth. And if nothing is true, then how do we define good and evil? Justice? Love? Respect?

A world without truth is a world without anchors. And when storms hit—and they always do—you need something solid to hold onto.

Wisdom *isn't just knowing that truth exists, it's choosing to live by it when others pretend it doesn't.*

What Jesus Said About Truth

Jesus didn't say, "Believe whatever makes you happy." He said:

"I am the way, the truth, and the life." — *John 14:6*

Notice that. He didn't claim to be *a* truth. He claimed to be **the** truth. That's bold. It's not always popular, but real truth usually isn't.

He also said:

"You will know the truth, and the truth will set you free."
— *John 8:32*

Freedom doesn't come from avoiding truth, it comes from embracing it. Living by truth doesn't limit you. It actually gives you clarity, purpose, and direction when everything else gets blurry.

Real Teen Example: Ella from Westfield, MA
Ella's English class had a unit on "exploring your personal truth." Students were encouraged to write essays that celebrated whatever made them feel good or powerful. Ella felt something was off. Instead of writing about her emotions, she submitted an essay titled *"Why Truth Isn't About Me."* She quoted Scripture, challenged the idea that everyone gets to define their own truth, and defended her belief in objective morality. She got a B... but her teacher pulled her aside afterward and said, "You've got guts. I don't agree with you, but I respect you."

Bold Defender: Chuck Colson (1931–2012)
Colson was once a top aide to President Nixon—ruthless, powerful, and ready to do anything to win. After the Watergate scandal took him down, he found Christ. His life turned upside down. He started a prison ministry and spent the rest of his life fighting for truth in culture, especially in law and politics. His message was clear: truth isn't about power, it's about serving something bigger than yourself.

Your Takeaways

You're going to hear a thousand versions of truth out there. Some will be clever. Some will sound kind. But when it comes to how you live, love, and lead, it all comes down to **what's real.**

Don't settle for what's trendy. Don't get tricked into thinking truth is just a vibe.
Stand on the truth that's been tested, proven, and unshaken:

Jesus doesn't offer a version of truth; **He is the truth.**

Jesus wasn't just saying He *tells* the truth; He was saying, **He *is* the truth**.

In other words:

- He's not just one opinion out of many.
- He's not a trend, a theory, or a TikTok influencer with hot takes.
- He's the **standard,** the **starting point** for what's real, what's right, and what lasts.

Imagine It Like This:

If life is a math test, and everyone's guessing the answers...

Jesus isn't just a student with the right answers, **He's the answer key.**

If life is a map and people are lost...
Jesus isn't just a tour guide,
He's the compass.

What Jesus means...If you want to know what's real, what's right, and what matters, **you start with Me.**

And that's a bold claim. Because if Jesus is the truth, then:

- You don't have to invent your identity
- You don't have to chase 20 opinions
- You have something solid when the world keeps changing

Chapter 15: "Don't Judge Me" — What Judgment Really Means

"Don't judge me."
"Only God can judge."
"You do you."

It's the most quoted command from people who've never opened a Bible. In today's culture, judgment is treated like the ultimate sin, especially if you're standing up for truth.

What Jesus Actually Said

"Do not judge, or you too will be judged." (Matthew 7:1)

But He also said:

"First take the plank out of your own eye, and then you will see clearly to remove the speck from your brother's eye." (Matthew 7:5)

Jesus is warning against **hypocritical judgment:** condemning others for sins or faults while ignoring your own. His message is: *Judge carefully, humbly, and by the same standard you'd want others to judge you.*

The issue is arrogance, not accountability.

Wisdom tells us when to speak and how to speak, so our correction builds others up instead of tearing them down. When someone's headed for danger, silence isn't love. It's abandonment.

Real Teen Example: Ethan from Dallas, Texas
Jordan, a junior in Nevada, saw a classmate post a racist joke online. Most kids just scrolled by. Jordan didn't. He replied, "That's not funny. It's not okay." His comment sparked

backlash: some laughed, others defended the post. But later, a quiet student messaged him privately: "Thanks for speaking up. I didn't know how." Jordan didn't go looking for a fight. He just knew staying silent wasn't right.

Judging Isn't the Problem

Judging with arrogance? That's the problem.
Judging with integrity and courage? That's the solution.

Truth without love becomes harsh.
Love without truth becomes hollow.

Our generation is drowning in the idea that "kindness means silence." But real kindness is honest even when it costs something.

Bold Defender:
Dietrich Bonhoeffer was a pastor in Nazi Germany. As Hitler rose to power, most churches went quiet, hoping to avoid trouble. Bonhoeffer didn't. He exposed evil from the pulpit and even helped lead resistance efforts. Arrested and eventually executed, he never backed down. One of his final writings said:

"Silence in the face of evil is itself evil."
Bonhoeffer didn't speak out because he hated people. He spoke out because he loved truth more than comfort—and people more than popularity.

When being judgmental is a moral responsibility
It's not about looking down on others. It's about **having the courage to name what's harmful, dishonest, or unjust**—and doing it because you care.

Think of it this way:

- If someone's spreading lies about a classmate and you stay silent, you're protecting the liar.

- If a friend is headed down a dangerous path and you say nothing, you're letting them fall.

- If a culture celebrates what's destructive, and no one speaks up, the damage spreads.

In those moments, being judgmental isn't mean, **it's necessary.**
It's not about being harsh, it's about **standing for truth when it counts.**

Silence is easy.
Judgment, when done right, is **character in action.**

Your Takeaways

You weren't made to stay silent.
You were made to stand for something.

Call out your own flaws first, but don't stop there.
Speak truth with humility. Stand for what's right with courage.

Judging isn't the problem.
Cowardice is.

Chapter 16: When Being "Nice" Isn't Enough

You've been told to be nice. Smile. Be agreeable. Don't rock the boat. Keep the peace.

But here's the truth: **nice isn't always good, and it's definitely not always right.**

Nice avoids conflict.
Character steps into it.

Nice wants to fit in.
Character is willing to stand out.

Jesus wasn't crucified because He was "nice." He was crucified because He told the truth, even when it made people angry.

There's a difference between being kind and being soft.
Kindness tells the truth in love.
Niceness stays silent to avoid tension.

Jesus didn't say, *"Blessed are the nice."*
He said:

"Blessed are those who are persecuted for righteousness' sake." (Matthew 5:10)

In a culture that rewards surface-level smiles and punishes deep convictions, teens today are being trained to choose comfort over courage.

Wisdom *draws the line between peacekeeping and truth-speaking because being kind doesn't mean being silent.*

Real Teen Example: Madison, from Norman, OK
Madison was in a club at school that promoted "positive

thinking." But one day, the leader announced they were going to start reading affirmations that contradicted her beliefs, saying things like "truth is whatever you decide it is."

Madison could've stayed quiet. Instead, she politely stood and said, "I believe truth is real, not relative. I can't participate in this." She didn't yell. She didn't shame anyone. But she didn't fake agreement either. She walked out alone and never regretted it.

When Kindness Isn't Quiet

Kindness is *not* the same as approval.

Approving of lies, just to avoid offending someone, is **not kindness, it's compromise.**
You can speak truth *and* show respect.
You can disagree *and* still love.

Culture says: "If you don't agree, you're hateful."
Jesus says: "Speak the truth in love." (Ephesians 4:15)

The strongest people aren't the loudest. They're the ones who stay calm, hold their ground, and don't back down from what's right.

Bold Defender:
Brayden worked at a summer job where his coworkers constantly told crude jokes and pressured him to laugh along. For a while, he did. But one day, something crossed the line. Instead of laughing, he said, "Hey, that's not funny. That's messed up." The group went quiet. Some rolled their eyes. One even said, "Lighten up." But afterward, one guy came up to him and said, "I respect that. I felt the same way." Brayden didn't win the crowd, but he found his voice.

Courage Is Louder Than Niceness

We've got enough people trying to be liked.

What we need are people who are brave enough to stand for truth and goodness, even when it makes them stand out in a dark or confused world.

Being nice keeps peace on the outside.
Being courageous creates peace on the inside.

If Jesus had only cared about being liked, He would've avoided the cross.
Instead, He walked right into it—for truth. For love. For you.

Your Takeaways

The world needs more than nice.
It needs you to be bold, humble, and real.

Don't fake agreement. Don't water down truth. Don't blend in just to survive.

You weren't made to be nice. You were made to be good.
And goodness, the kind that stands when others sit, **always makes a difference.**

Chapter 17: Standing Alone Without Feeling Alone

No one likes being the only one.
The only one not laughing at the joke.
The only one not reposting the meme.
The only one who says, *"That's not right."*

It's awkward. It's lonely. Sometimes it even feels pointless.

But here's what you need to know:
You might stand alone, but you're never truly alone.

God doesn't just see it. He honors it.

The Courage to Be the First

Every bold movement starts with one person deciding to stop waiting for backup.

It's tempting to think, *"I'll speak up once someone else does."* But often, no one else will until you go first.

Real Teen Example – Elijah, 15, from Huntsville, AL
Elijah was the only one in his friend group who refused to download an app known for its toxic content. When others mocked him and said, "You're overthinking it," he held his ground. Months later, that same app was exposed for spreading explicit material. One of the guys who mocked him came back and said, "You were right. I wish I hadn't signed up." Elijah wasn't trying to be better. He was just trying to stay clean. He stood alone, but not in vain.

Wisdom *sees beyond the moment, knowing today's lonely stand might become tomorrow's example of courage.*

When You Feel Surrounded

There's a story in 2 Kings 6 where Elisha's servant sees an enemy army and panics. He says, *"What are we going to do?"* But Elisha calmly replies,

"Don't be afraid. Those who are with us are more than those who are with them."
And God opens the servant's eyes to see **angels surrounding them**—an army of fire, standing guard.

You might feel outnumbered at school, online, even in your own family.
But you're not outnumbered.
You just haven't seen the army yet.

Bold Example: Timothée Chalamet
He's one of the most recognizable actors of his generation, but he doesn't chase attention to stay in the spotlight. He chooses his roles carefully, speaks with thoughtfulness, and carries himself with humility in an industry built on noise. He's shown that confidence doesn't always look like domination, it can look like quiet focus and self-respect. In interviews, he's calm. In his choices, he's intentional. He doesn't need to shout to stand out. And that's the lesson: **Character doesn't compete for attention. It just keeps showing up.**

The Power of One

You're not called to win the crowd.
You're called to be consistent.

In a world chasing clicks and likes, standing alone might feel like failure. But in God's eyes, it's **faithfulness,** and He multiplies it.

Moses stood alone at the Red Sea.
Daniel stood alone in Babylon.
Jesus stood alone in front of Pilate.

When you stand with God, you're never out of place even if you're out of step with everyone else.

Your Takeaways

Standing alone isn't easy. But it's **worth it.**

Every time you choose truth over popularity, you make it easier for the next person to do the same.

The world needs someone to go first.
Someone to light the match.
Someone to draw the line.
Why not you?

Chapter 18: Strength Isn't Always Loud

Some people think boldness means being loud, aggressive, or always having the last word.

But the strongest people don't always raise their voices. Sometimes, real strength shows up in the quiet moments, when you choose restraint over reaction, clarity over chaos.

It's not weakness to speak the truth quietly. It's wisdom.

Quiet Strength Is Still Strength

And it's wisdom because:

- **Wisdom knows timing.** It chooses when to speak and when to stay silent, not out of fear, but out of purpose.

- **Wisdom knows tone.** It doesn't shout to be heard; it speaks clearly so others want to listen.

- **Wisdom isn't about winning arguments, it's about shaping hearts.** And hearts don't change when they feel attacked. They change when they feel convicted.

So when someone speaks the truth calmly and confidently, they're not being timid.
They're showing the maturity to **stand for something** without letting noise define the moment.

Loud Isn't the Same as Right

Some of the most dangerous people in history shouted their beliefs.

And some of the wisest ones spoke with gentleness and still changed the world.

Wisdom teaches you when to speak and when silence speaks louder.

Volume doesn't make truth more true.
And silence doesn't always mean surrender.
What matters is the **heart behind the words** and the **strength to hold your ground without shoving others down**.

Real Teen Example – Elijah, 16, from Harrisburg, Pennsylvania

Elijah was in a youth group where heated debates broke out over politics. While others raised their voices, Elijah simply said, "We should care more about people than being right." The room got quiet. He didn't dominate the conversation, he redirected it. Weeks later, someone told him, "You didn't say much, but I remember what you said. And it stuck." He didn't win the argument. He led with calm clarity.

Still Waters Run Deep

It's easy to explode.
It's easy to get loud.
It's harder to be steady, to speak truth when needed, and be silent when it's wise.

There's a reason Proverbs says:

"A gentle answer turns away wrath, but a harsh word stirs up anger." (Proverbs 15:1)

It's not about being soft.
It's about being effective.

Bold Defender: Zendaya

Zendaya doesn't lead with drama or volume, she leads with presence. From Disney Channel to blockbuster films, she's built her career with quiet consistency, strong choices, and grace under pressure. She doesn't chase controversy to stay relevant. She lets her work, her character, and her confidence speak for her. In interviews, she's calm. In criticism, she's composed. In a culture obsessed with attention, Zendaya reminds us that **you don't have to be loud to make a difference.**

Strength doesn't always look like shouting. Sometimes, it looks like showing up, staying steady, and choosing character again and again.

Your Takeaways

The world will tell you that louder is stronger.
But sometimes, the strongest voice in the room is the one that doesn't need to shout.

When you speak truth with calm and unwavering confidence, you show strength that noise can't touch.
That's not weakness. That's wisdom.

Taylor Swift once said, "Silence speaks so much louder than screaming tantrums. Never give anyone an excuse to say that you're crazy." For someone constantly in the spotlight, she's learned how to speak up with class, set boundaries with courage, and walk away when necessary. She's re-recorded her entire music catalog to reclaim what was hers, not for revenge, but for ownership. That's not just business. That's conviction.

You don't have to be famous to do the same. You just have to know what's right and stand for it, even when it's easier to go quiet.

Chapter 19: What You Laugh At, You Learn From

Laughter is powerful.

It can bring people together.
Break the tension.
Even heal pain.

But it can also shape you without you realizing it.

Every joke carries a message. Every meme has a moral. Every laugh teaches you something **about what's okay, what's cool, and what doesn't matter.**

If you're not paying attention, you'll end up laughing at the very things you should be standing against.

The Hidden Curriculum of Comedy

Think about it.

- A show makes fun of purity, and suddenly it's "outdated."

- A skit mocks faith, and now it's "weird."

- A meme turns cheating into a joke, and people call it "relatable."

The more you laugh, the less serious it feels. And over time, the edge wears off your convictions.

What once made you uncomfortable...now makes you chuckle.
What once felt wrong...now just feels normal.

Laughter is a teacher. Be careful who's doing the teaching.

Real Teen Example – Laila, 16, from Corning, New York

Laila used to watch a late-night comedy show every week. It was clever, fast, and funny. But over time, she realized something: every episode made fun of people who believed in God. Always with a smirk. Always with a punchline. One day, she asked herself, "Why am I laughing at something that matters to me?" She stopped watching. "It wasn't that I became offended," she said. "I just decided I wasn't going to let jokes rewrite what I believe."

There's Nothing Funny About Losing Yourself

Humor isn't harmless when it chips away at your values.
When it softens your spine.
When it teaches you to laugh at what once made you strong.

You don't have to be bitter.
You don't have to cancel anyone.
But you do have to draw a line.

Stand For Something even if it means you stop laughing when everyone else keeps going.

Bold Defender – Diego, 17, from Springfield, Illinois

Diego and his friends followed a popular YouTube creator known for outrageous pranks and edgy humor. But one day, the jokes crossed a line, mocking disabled students at a school. Most people laughed it off. Diego didn't. He commented, "This isn't funny. It's cruel." The backlash came quickly—DMs, insults, even friends teasing him. But weeks later, someone quietly messaged him: "Thanks for saying something. I thought it was wrong too." Diego didn't set out to be the moral police. He just refused to laugh at cruelty.

The Joke's On You If You Don't Choose

You don't need to be hyper-serious all the time. But you *do* need to stay sharp.

Pay attention to what makes you laugh.
Because over time, your laughter becomes your approval.
And your approval shapes your character.

Your Takeaways

Laughter is a gift.
But it can also be a trap.

You're not weak for walking away from jokes that cheapen who you are.
You're not boring for saying, "That's not funny."

You're choosing to stand for something.
And that's always worth more than a laugh.

Wisdom *watches what entertains you because what you laugh at today could shape what you tolerate tomorrow.*

Chapter 20: The World's Approval Isn't Worth Your Soul

Let's be real, **everyone wants to be liked.**

It feels good to be noticed.
It feels powerful to be praised.
And it feels easy to go with the crowd.

But here's the danger: if you live for the world's approval, you'll constantly trade truth for applause and **you'll lose who you are trying to please everyone else.**

The world changes its mind every day.
What's "cool" today gets canceled tomorrow.
If you're chasing acceptance, you'll never rest and you'll never be free.

The High Cost of Being Liked

Jesus said:

"What good is it for someone to gain the whole world, yet forfeit their soul?" (Mark 8:36)

You can be famous and empty.
Popular and miserable.
Surrounded and still be deeply alone.

That's the trap of worldly approval: it promises everything and delivers nothing.

Wisdom *reminds us that the applause of the world fades, but a life of character leaves an echo that lasts.*

Real Teen Example – Jaden, 17, from Colorado Springs, CO
Jaden went viral on TikTok for doing challenges that pushed boundaries. His follower count exploded. But inside, he felt

fake. He said, "I was doing stuff I didn't even believe in just for views." Eventually, he posted a video explaining why he was stepping away. He lost thousands of followers in one night. But he said, "For the first time in months, I slept well. I felt clean." He walked away from the world's approval to find peace and his real voice.

Chasing Crowds Is a Trap

If you shape your life around other people's opinions, you'll end up with **a life that doesn't look anything like you.**

The world is loud.
But so is your soul if you take the time to listen.

Stand For Something even when the crowd moves on without you.

Example #2 – Nevaeh, 15, from Orlando, Florida
Nevaeh was voted "most liked" in her class and had the biggest Snapchat streak in school. But what people didn't know was that she cried almost every night. "I was terrified of messing up," she said. "If I said the wrong thing, it was over." One day, she deleted her streaks, unfollowed some toxic people, and started journaling instead. "I stopped performing and started becoming," she said. "Now I'm not the most liked, but I'm finally real."

Be Known for the Right Things

God didn't create you to blend in.

He created you to shine, **not for attention, but for impact.**

Put another way, the world will accommodate you for fitting in, but it will only reward you for standing out.

Don't settle for likes when you're called to live for something eternal.
Popularity fades. Purpose doesn't.

Your Takeaways

You don't need the world's approval to live a good life.
You need truth. Integrity. Conviction.

Stand For Something because your soul is worth more than a spotlight.

"When wealth is lost, nothing is lost; when health is lost, something is lost; when character is lost, all is lost."
—Billy Graham

Chapter 21: Courage Isn't Loud, But It's Real

We live in a world that mistakes volume for strength.
Whoever shouts the loudest, posts the boldest, or sparks the biggest reaction is seen as the one with "courage."

But real courage? It's usually quiet.
It doesn't demand attention.
It doesn't need a stage.

It simply stands when everyone else sits.

Quiet Doesn't Mean Weak

Some of the most courageous people you'll ever meet won't raise their voice.
They'll raise their standards.

They won't push their views on others.
They'll **live** them consistently, humbly, without apology.

Jesus wasn't always loud. But He was always brave.
He spoke truth with calm conviction, even when it put a target on His back.

Wisdom *is knowing when to stand up and when to stand still.*
Courage without wisdom can become noise.

Courage isn't noise. Courage is *not backing down*.

Real Teen Example – Naomi, 14, from Saginaw, Michigan
When Naomi's history teacher asked the class to write an

essay about "why religion causes more harm than good," she felt her stomach sink. But instead of writing what the teacher seemed to want, she respectfully disagreed. She wrote about the good her faith had done in her life and in the world. She got a lower grade. But when a few students read her essay later, one said, "That's the first time I've heard someone actually stand up for what they believe in." Naomi didn't win the grade. She won something better.

The World Respects Quiet Strength (Even If It Pretends Not To)

You don't have to yell.
You don't have to argue.
You just have to be unshaken.

Stand For Something with quiet confidence, not loud insecurity.

Courage isn't about drawing attention. It's about **holding the line** when it counts.

Bold Defender – Isaiah, 16, from Raleigh, North Carolina
Isaiah was on the basketball team. The locker room wasn't exactly a place for deep values. But when the team started joking about girls in graphic ways, he didn't laugh. He didn't argue either. He just stood, grabbed his bag, and walked out. Later, one teammate told him, "You made it awkward, man." But another whispered, "Thanks. I didn't know how to get out of there either." Isaiah didn't yell. He just moved, and his character spoke louder than words.

Don't Mistake Flash for Fire.

The world praises bold personalities.
But God honors bold **character**.

Courage might not trend.
But it will be remembered.

Your Takeaways

You don't need a microphone to make an impact.
You need conviction.

Stand For Something even if you stand in silence.
Because courage isn't always loud. But it's always real

"Courage is the first of human qualities because it is the quality which guarantees the others."
— *Aristotle*

Chapter 22: You Weren't Made to Fit In

Let's get this out of the way:

You're not supposed to fit in.

You weren't designed to disappear into the crowd, to blend into the noise, or to shrink yourself just to avoid attention.
You were made to stand out with purpose. With clarity. With character.

Fitting in feels safe until you realize you've lost yourself in the process.

There's a Reason You Feel the Tension

If you're a believer trying to live with integrity, there will always be moments when you feel out of sync with the world around you.

That's not failure. That's confirmation.

The goal isn't comfort, it's calling.

Wisdom *isn't about hiding your light, it's about knowing how to shine it without burning bridges.*

You weren't created to blend. You were created to be a **light**. And light, by definition, **doesn't fit in with darkness.**

Real Teen Example – Caleb, 15, from Jefferson City, Missouri
Caleb transferred to a public high school after years in a small Christian school. At first, he tried to

fit in, laughing at jokes he didn't like, staying quiet when things crossed the line. But it ate at him. One day, he just stopped pretending. He lost friends, sure. But he found peace. "I'd rather walk alone than lie to fit in," he said. His new friends are fewer, but genuine and real.

Your Difference Is Your Strength

God made you distinct on purpose.
Not to isolate you, but to **use you**.

If the world doesn't understand you, that doesn't mean something's wrong. It may just mean something's right.

Stand For Something, especially when the world pressures you to stand down.

The world doesn't need more copies.
It needs originals who live with truth and courage.

Bold Defender – Tiana, 17, from Hershey, Pennsylvania
Tiana was the only girl in her friend group who didn't party. They teased her at first. "Come on, live a little," they'd say. But she never budged. "It's not about rules," she told them. "It's about respect for myself and my future." Months later, one of those girls came to her in tears after a rough night and said, "I wish I had your strength." Tiana didn't need to fit in to matter, her difference made her dependable.

Fit In or Stand Out, You Can't Do Both

There's nothing brave about blending in.
There's nothing admirable about compromise.

You don't have to be obnoxious.
But you do have to be anchored.

Your Takeaways

Don't trade who you are just to be accepted by people who don't really know you.

You were made to live bold.
To walk with conviction.
To shine in dark places.

Stand For Something, and never apologize for being different.

Chapter 23: Don't Confuse Freedom With Chaos

Freedom is a gift. But **freedom isn't the same thing as doing whatever you want.**

That's not freedom. That's chaos.

Culture keeps shouting, *"Be free!"*
But if freedom means ignoring truth, ditching responsibility, and erasing boundaries, then what you're left with isn't liberty, it's **wreckage**.

Not every path looks free leads somewhere.

Real freedom doesn't mean no rules.
It means the **right rules**, chosen on purpose.

Boundaries Don't Trap You, They Protect You

A train is only free when it stays on the tracks.
The second it jumps the rails, it crashes.

Same with your life.

Freedom works best when it's anchored to **truth**, not impulse.
To **purpose**, not popularity.

Wisdom *teaches that real freedom has form. Without boundaries, freedom becomes a trap.*

Real Teen Example – Zeke, 17, from Winnebago, KS
Zeke used to think following rules meant giving up his freedom. So he did whatever he felt like: skipping class, partying, lying to cover it up. "I thought I was living," he said.

"But I was just drifting." It caught up with him fast. A suspension. A breakup. A reputation he didn't want. It took a

mentor to help him see: freedom without direction leads to regret. He turned it around, but it started when he stopped calling chaos freedom.

The Lie of "Do Whatever Feels Right"

It sounds empowering.
But it's actually enslaving because your feelings **change by the hour.**

If freedom means chasing every urge, you'll be exhausted and empty.
If it means being rooted in truth, you'll be steady even when life shakes you.

Stand For Something, or you'll fall for every impulse dressed up as liberation.

Bold Defender – Kennedy, 16, from Portland, Oregon
Kennedy's friends told her she was "too intense" for having standards. She didn't sleep around, didn't drink, and didn't feel bad about it. "I'm not uptight," she'd say. "I just know what I want my future to look like." One night, after a party, one of the same friends who had mocked her texted: *"I wish I had your self-control."* Kennedy wasn't trying to impress anyone. She just knew **freedom meant living on purpose**, not reacting to pressure.

Real Freedom Comes From the Inside

It's not about more options.
It's about deeper roots.

You don't need to chase chaos to prove you're free.
You need to choose what matters and **stay steady,** especially when everything else feels out of control.

Your Takeaways

You weren't made to drift.
You were made to decide.

Stand For Something because freedom without truth will leave you lost.

Chapter 24: Truth Isn't Trendy, and That's The Point

Let's be honest: **truth is out of style.**

Today's world celebrates feelings, preferences, and opinions, but if you dare to say, *"This is true,"* you'll get labeled as judgmental, intolerant, or worse.

But truth doesn't need a fan club.
It doesn't need to trend.
It just needs people who are willing to stand for something even when it's unpopular.

Truth Doesn't Expire

Trends come and go.
Today's "new idea" becomes tomorrow's punchline.
But truth? It doesn't age. It holds steadily even when the world spins fast.

Jesus didn't say:

"You'll feel your truth."
He said:
"You will know the truth, and the truth will set you free." (John 8:32)

Truth doesn't adapt to culture.
Culture should adjust to truth.

Wisdom *isn't trendy either. It holds truth steadily even when everyone else wavers.*

Real Teen Example #1 – Mariah, 15, from Washington, DC
Mariah was in a class where they were asked to write a paper on why all beliefs are equally true. She felt torn. But she

respectfully explained why she believed some things are actually **right or wrong,** not just opinion. She didn't bash others. She just stood by her view. Her grade dropped a bit, but something else happened: two classmates asked to talk after class. One said, "I don't agree with you, but I respect you." Mariah didn't preach. She just refused to fold.

Truth Isn't Popular, It's Permanent

You don't follow truth like it's a trend.
You follow it like it's your compass.

And that means **you'll feel alone sometimes** because most people are following feelings instead.

But when you stand for something that doesn't shift with the wind, you become someone others can actually trust. And look up to.

Bold Defender: Sadie Robertson Huff
Sadie Robertson Huff doesn't just talk about character, she lives it. As a speaker, author, and young mom, she's built a platform not by blending in, but by standing out with joy, honesty, and faith. She talks openly about insecurity, temptation, and staying rooted in truth in a world that constantly pushes compromise. "You weren't made to blend in," she says. "You were made to stand out for the right reasons." And she's right. Influence doesn't come from noise. It comes from knowing who you are, and living like it matters. That's what real character looks like.

What You Believe Shapes What You Become

You can't live a life of strength while standing on weak ideas. You need a foundation that doesn't shift every time culture updates its opinions.

You don't need the world to agree with you.
You just need the conviction to stand for something that won't collapse under pressure.

Your Takeaways

Truth may not trend.
But it always wins in the end.

It doesn't shout. It doesn't panic.
But it never changes and never leaves you guessing.

Stand for something that lasts because everything else is already fading.

Culture Education vs Christian Education

Culture Teaches	Christian Education Offers
Truth is personal	Truth is unchanging
Identity is self-defined	Identity is God-given
Success is self-glory	Success is stewardship
History is random	History reveals God's hand

Chapter 25: Being Offended Doesn't Make You Right

We live in a time when everyone is ready to be offended. It's almost a badge of honor now, like the more sensitive you are, the more "aware" you must be.

But here's the truth:

Feeling offended doesn't make you right.

Sometimes it means you're paying attention.
Other times it means you're avoiding growth.

Offense Is a Reaction, Not a Reason

The world teaches you to speak your truth unless your truth makes someone uncomfortable. Then you're told to be quiet.

But being uncomfortable isn't a bad thing.
In fact, truth often **starts** with discomfort.

Jesus offended people all the time, not by being cruel, but by being **clear**. For example, in John 8:58, Jesus says, *"Before Abraham was, I am."*

Wisdom *knows that offense can be a mirror, not a weapon. It reveals more about the hearer than the speaker.*

By using the divine name **"I am,"** He wasn't just making a theological point, He was directly claiming to be God. The religious leaders were so offended by His **clarity** that they picked up stones to kill Him.

He wasn't rude.
He wasn't mocking.
He was just clear, and it shook them to the core.

Real Teen Example – Levi, 17, from Reno, Nevada
Levi was asked to share during a classroom discussion on gender identity. He calmly stated that he believes gender is rooted in biology. No shouting. No jokes. Just his belief. One student stormed out. The teacher looked uneasy. Later that day, Levi got an email asking him to "reconsider" his comments. He replied respectfully: "Disagreeing isn't hate. I spoke kindly, and I'll continue to do so." He didn't shrink back just because someone else was offended. He chose to stand for something without being harsh.

Truth and Kindness Can Coexist

You don't have to choose between truth and kindness.
You can be clear without being cruel.
You can be strong without being sarcastic.

Let others be quick to take offense. You stay steady.

In a culture that glorifies outrage, choose to **stand for something** quietly and confidently because the goal isn't to avoid offense, it's to speak with love and clarity even when the truth stings.

Bold Defender – Sierra, 16, from Hartford, CT
Sierra was mentoring a younger girl through her church when the girl shared she was watching shows full of dark themes and demonic content. Sierra gently said, "I think you should be careful about what you let in." The girl got defensive and stopped texting her. Weeks later, Sierra received a message: "You were right. I had nightmares and

felt weird. I deleted it all. Thanks for caring enough to speak up." Sierra knew the risk, but she also knew silence wasn't love.

You Can't Grow If You Can't Be Challenged

The truth isn't always easy to hear.
But it's what helps us mature, rise, and become who we're meant to be.

If you're never challenged, you'll never change.

Your Takeaways

Don't confuse truth with hate.
Don't mistake comfort for clarity.

If what you believe makes someone uncomfortable, that doesn't mean you're wrong.
It just means you're **awake** and possibly on to something real.

Stand for something even when others would rather you sit down.

Chapter 26: Conviction Isn't Hate

This culture loves to blur lines.

If you believe in something deeply, especially something moral or biblical, **you're told you're hateful.**
The message is clear:

- If you disagree, you're dangerous.

- If you take a stand, you're the problem.

But that's not truth. That's control.

Conviction is not hate.
And real love isn't soft silence, it's **honest courage.**

Disagreement Doesn't Equal Disrespect

You can love someone and still say, *"I don't agree."*
That's not hateful. That's human.

Jesus did it constantly: He dined with sinners, defended the broken, and still called sin what it is. He showed compassion without compromising truth.

Conviction needs **wisdom** *so that truth is delivered with clarity, not cruelty.*

And He did it not to shame people, but to set them free.

Real Teen Example – Bella, 16, from Indianapolis, Indiana
Bella was part of a school club where a friend came out as nonbinary. Everyone applauded. Bella didn't. She didn't mock. She didn't protest. She just didn't cheer and later told her friend privately, "I care about you, but I believe identity is something God defines." The friend pulled away for a while. But months later, they started texting again. This time with questions about faith. Bella didn't have to argue. She just chose to stand for something without losing compassion.

Real Conviction Looks Like Stability

The world is full of emotional outbursts.
What it rarely sees and respects is quiet strength.

It's easier to go along with everything than to hold your ground without becoming bitter.

But if you stand for something solid, **you don't need to shout.** You just need to show up and stay true.

Bold Defender – Jason, 17, from Houston, Texas
Jason posted a Bible verse about purity on his Instagram story. The comments came fast: "Judgmental." "Religious freak." "Get real." He didn't delete it. He didn't respond with snark. He posted a second story the next day: *"Conviction isn't hate. It's love that won't lie."* A week later, two students messaged him privately thanking him for being consistent. "You gave me guts," one said. "I've been afraid to post what I believe."

You Can Be Bold Without Being Cruel

Holding conviction doesn't mean holding contempt.
You can be clear without being combative.
You can disagree without degrading.

And when you live that way long enough, even your critics take notice. They notice your values.
Wisdom protects your courage from turning into condemnation.

Your Takeaways

You don't need to be loud.
You don't need to be liked.

You just need to be steady, especially when others call your clarity offensive.
Because when you stand for something rooted in truth and led by love, you don't tear people down, you help hold the line for what matters.

What Is Character?

Character is a commitment to a set of values that never change.

That's why numbers and letters are called characters—because they don't shift. They don't bend to pressure. They don't change with opinion.

In a world that constantly redefines what's right, real character stays fixed. It's not about being perfect.

It's about being anchored to something that doesn't move—especially when everything else does.

Chapter 27: You Don't Need Everyone to Like You

Let's say it plainly: **you won't be liked by everyone, and you're not supposed to be.**

If you're living with conviction, clarity, and character, **some people will pull back.**
Not because you're rude, but because your presence reminds them of what they're avoiding.

Approval Is a Moving Target

Wisdom *reminds you: if you chase everyone's approval, you'll lose your direction.*

To get everyone to like you is exhausting.
One day they cheer you. The next they ghost you.
Live like that long enough, and you'll shape-shift into whatever the moment demands until you don't even recognize yourself anymore.

But when you **stand for something meaningful**, you stop chasing approval.
You start living with focus.

Real Teen Example – Alexis, 15, from Burlington, VT
Alexis was part of a large friend group until she started posting more about her faith. Slowly, the invites stopped coming. At first, she panicked and tried to "tone it down." But after praying, she leaned in instead. She began sharing more—honestly, gently. A year later, she has fewer friends,

but they're solid. "I lost the crowd," she said, "but I found my people."

You're Not Rejected, You're Refined

When people back away because of your beliefs, don't let it harden you.
But don't let it shake you either.

They're not always rejecting *you*.
They're retreating from the **reminder** of something deeper.

And that's okay.

Real relationships don't require you to mute your convictions. They grow when you're **clear about what matters.**

Example #2 – Noah, 18, from Moab, UT

Noah was the only one in his friend group who didn't go along with the senior prank. "It was funny," he said, "but it was also stupid and illegal." He caught flak for it. "You think you're better than us?" one classmate said. Noah just shrugged. "No. I just don't think wrecking things is character." Later, a teacher pulled him aside: "Thanks for standing up. You reminded me that leadership still exists."

Likeability Is a Trap

Be kind. Be respectful. But don't bend yourself into someone else's mold just to avoid tension.

When you live anchored to truth, some people will walk away.

Let them.

You don't need everyone.
You just need the courage to **be consistent** when it counts.

Your Takeaway

Chapter 28: Don't Trade Clarity for Acceptance

You've probably felt it.

That moment when you're about to speak up, but pause. Not because you don't know what's true. But because you're not sure **how it'll land**.

It's tempting to water things down just to keep the peace. But there's a cost to silence. And there's a bigger cost to **compromise**.

What You Compromise to Get, You'll Compromise to Keep

Wisdom shows you where clarity ends and compromise begins.

If you edit your convictions just to gain approval, you'll have to keep editing to hold onto it.
It becomes a cycle of shrinking, silencing, and surrendering.

But when you **stand for something clear and true**, you can live freely even if it costs you popularity.

Real Teen Example – Isaiah, 17, from Santa Fe, NM
Isaiah was accepted into a leadership program but was asked to sign a statement affirming "all perspectives as equally valid." He paused. Respectfully, he said, "I can respect people without agreeing with everything." He declined to sign and lost the spot. But a different program reached out later.

"Your integrity spoke louder than your résumé," they said.
There's a Difference Between Being Kind and Being Vague.

Kindness never requires you to hide the truth.
Real kindness is honest, but respectful.

You don't have to yell. You don't have to argue.
But you do have to **draw a line,** not in anger, but in clarity.

Because every time you choose clarity over comfort, you build the kind of character that lasts.

Bold Defender – Zoe, 16, from New York

Zoe was part of her school's peer mentoring team. When asked to lead a workshop on "gender identity and fluid morality," she asked for permission to opt out. "I don't want to offend anyone," she said, "but I also can't teach something I don't believe." She was quietly removed from the team. But a younger student later thanked her: "I thought I was the only one." That day, Zoe stood alone, but she stood for something that mattered.

If you want to see what it really looks like to stand for truth—at great personal cost—watch this most powerful movie, *A Man for All Seasons.*
It's the true story of Sir Thomas More, who chose not to betray his conscience under any circumstance.

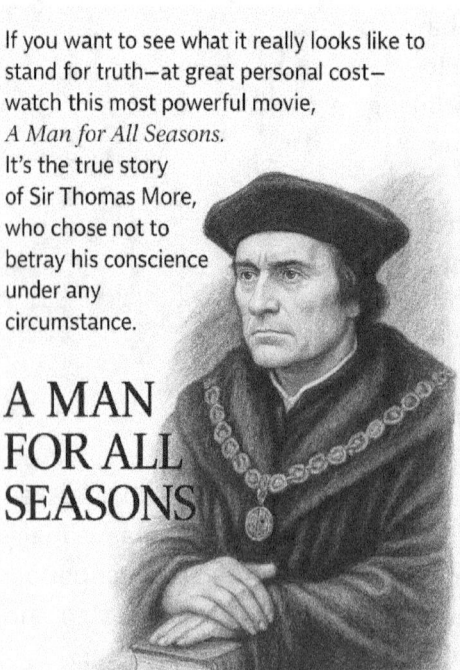

Your Takeaways

It's easy to blend in.
It's harder to be clear.

But if you keep trading clarity for acceptance, you'll eventually lose both.

Truth doesn't need to be loud, but it does need to be lived.

Chapter 29: Courage Isn't Loud Either

Courage is often misunderstood.

It's not always running into danger or shouting down opposition.
Sometimes it's choosing to **still show up,** to walk into a room, a classroom, a friend group, knowing they might not accept your faith, but you carry it anyway.

You don't need to draw attention to yourself.
But you don't need to hide, either.

Courage Isn't a Roar, It's a Resolve

The bravest people aren't always the boldest voices.
They're often the ones who show up with quiet faith and **refuse to flinch**.

They don't need a stage.
They don't need applause.
They just know what they believe, and they live it anyway.

Wisdom *helps you choose when to speak and when to stand in silence, and both take courage.*

That's what it means to **stand for something** without performing for the crowd.

Real Teen Example – Daniel, 17, from Jackson, MS
Daniel kept a Bible in his backpack. One day it fell out during gym. A group of students started laughing and called him "pastor boy." Daniel could've laughed it off or stayed silent. Instead, he picked it up and said, "Yeah, that's mine."

No lecture. No defense. Just ownership. That moment sparked a conversation days later with a classmate who had questions

about God. "It mattered," the classmate told him. "You didn't run."

Real Courage Doesn't Look for a Fight

Some people confuse being confrontational with being courageous.
But courage isn't about pushing people around.
It's about **refusing to be pushed out** of who you are.

You don't have to wear a sign.
You just have to **keep showing up** with conviction.

Even when it costs you comfort.

Even when no one claps.

Bold Defender – Hannah, 15, from Columbia, South Carolina

Hannah was cast in a school play with a scene she wasn't comfortable performing. She politely asked the director if she could sit that part out. The director said no. So Hannah stepped down from the role. Some classmates rolled their eyes. One even told her, "You're ruining the show." But a teacher quietly pulled her aside later and said, "You showed more strength than most adults I know."

Your Takeaways

You don't need the spotlight to be brave.
You just need the courage to keep showing up, unshaken.

Because in a world that pressures you to shrink, the boldest move might be to **just stand your ground without saying a word.**

Chapter 30: You're Not Who They Say You Are

Culture is loud about identity.

It wants to define you by your looks, your likes, your labels, or your past.
And if you don't accept its version of who you are, you'll be told you're confused, or worse, dangerous.

But identity isn't something the world gives you.
It's something God already **gave** you.

Don't Let Labels Limit You

You're not too far gone.
You're not too small.
You're not "just" anything.

When you know **who you are in Christ**, you stop living for approval and start living with purpose. You don't need to fit anyone else's mold.

You can stand for something deeper than attention or applause.

Wisdom *grounds your identity in truth, not trends.*

Real Teen Example – Ava, 16, from Washington

Ava was always the quiet one. People assumed she had no opinions. But in English class, she spoke up when a teacher said, "There's no such thing as absolute truth." Calmly, Ava said, "Actually, I believe there is." A few students snickered, but the teacher nodded and moved on. After class, two classmates told her, "We've never heard you talk. But that was cool." Ava didn't need to be loud. She just needed to **stop letting the world's label define her.**

Know Who You Are Before They Tell You

If you don't decide who you are, someone else will.
And it won't be based on truth, it'll be based on trend.

The more grounded you are in truth, the less shaken you'll be by opinion.

Culture changes weekly. Truth doesn't.

And when you know where your identity comes from, you stop performing for approval.

Bold Defender – Marcus, 17, from Illinois
Marcus was labeled "trouble" since middle school. But sophomore year, he found faith and everything changed. He stopped vaping, stopped skipping, and started mentoring younger students. A former teacher asked him what happened. He said, "I realized I'm not who people say I am. I'm who God says I am." That mindset didn't erase his past. But it **refused to let his past define his future.**

✦ Your Takeaways

You're not a trend.
You're not a test score.
You're not a label.

You are **known**, **called**, and **capable** of living out your faith with strength even if no one claps for you.

Stand for something that won't change when the crowd turns.

Chapter 31: Opposition Doesn't Mean You're Wrong

The moment you take a stand, someone will try to push you back.
It's not a maybe, it's a guarantee.

You'll be told you're too intense.
Too narrow.
Too serious.
Too much.

But if you're standing for truth, you're not being too much.
You're being **faithful**.

Resistance Doesn't Equal Rejection

Not everyone will clap.
Not everyone will agree.
But pushback is often a sign that **what you're doing matters**.

You don't have to be combative.
You just have to be clear.

And when your clarity causes tension, **don't assume you're in the wrong**.

Real Teen Example – Chloe, 15, from Cleveland, Ohio

Chloe spoke at her school's open mic night and read a short poem about forgiveness and faith. The next day, someone tagged her in a post mocking it. Instead of deleting her account, she posted again: "You don't have to like it, but I won't apologize for believing it." Some unfollowed.

But others messaged her privately, saying, "I needed that." Opposition didn't silence her, it sharpened her voice.

Don't Let Criticism Shrink Your Conviction

You don't need to get defensive when criticized.
You don't need to argue with everyone who disagrees.
But you do need to **stay rooted** when others try to pull you off center.

Wisdom *is knowing when to speak, when to stand—and when to wait. Courage without wisdom can become noise. But together, they become strength with purpose.*

If the goal is to please everyone, you'll never live with peace. But if the goal is to honor truth, **peace will follow even in storms.**

Bold Defender – Jordan, 18, from Missouri

Jordan wore a shirt to school that said *"Truth > Trend."* A few students rolled their eyes. A teacher asked him to cover it up. He respectfully refused. "It's not hateful," he said. "It's just honest." He got sent to the office, but left the shirt on. Later that week, a younger student thanked him for not backing down. "You gave me courage to speak up too." Jordan didn't try to be a rebel. He just refused to be silenced.

✦ Your Takeaways

Criticism isn't always a warning sign.
Sometimes, it's a confirmation that you're exactly where you're supposed to be.

Stand for something, and you'll be misunderstood.
But keep standing, and you'll also be remembered and admired.

"It's not what happens to you, but how you react to it that matters."
> — *Epictetus (Greek philosopher)*

Chapter 32: You Can Be Bold Without Being Loud

Some people confuse boldness with volume.
But bold doesn't mean brash.
And confidence doesn't need a spotlight.

You can be bold by showing up, speaking truth, and staying kind even when no one else does.

That's not noise. That's power under control.

Wisdom *tames boldness. It doesn't silence it, it steers it. Without wisdom, boldness turns into arrogance. With wisdom, boldness earns respect.*

Boldness Is Clarity, Not Chaos

Real boldness is knowing what matters and not folding when it's tested.
You don't need to dominate a conversation to lead it.
You just need to **stand for something** and stay consistent.

Sometimes the boldest thing you can do is say,

"Here's what I believe. I'm not attacking you. I'm just not hiding it."

Real Teen Example – Kennedy, 17, from Ogden, Utah
Kennedy gave a presentation in her government class on free speech. She included faith-based examples respectfully, but clearly. One student said afterward, "That was pretty bold."

Kennedy smiled and said, "It wasn't meant to be bold. It was meant to be honest." That one line sparked a 30-minute after-class discussion with classmates who had never thought about faith from that angle.

Your Tone Can Be Calm And Still Be Strong

Don't confuse soft speech with weak conviction.
Jesus didn't yell to make His point.
He **asked questions, told stories, and lived what He taught,** and it shook the world.

Boldness isn't about taking up space.
It's about standing on truth even when it's inconvenient.

Bold Defender – Malik, 16, from New York
Malik wore a wristband that said "Truth Lives Here." A teacher told him to take it off. "Too political," she said. He politely asked what rule it broke. She couldn't find one. He kept wearing it. A week later, that same teacher asked, "What does it mean to you?" Malik answered, "It means I don't pretend truth changes just to fit in." She didn't agree—but she listened. Boldness didn't have to shout. It just had to show up.

✦ Your Takeaways

Being bold isn't about having the loudest voice.
It's about having the clearest one and not backing down when the world says, "Be quiet."

When you **stand for something,** people might call you intense.
Let them.
You don't need to raise your voice to be heard.
You just need to **mean every word.**

Chapter 33: You Don't Create Truth, You Align With It

We live in a world that says:

"Be your truth."
"Live your truth."
"Define your truth."

But truth doesn't bend just because we want it to.
It doesn't shift with feelings.
It doesn't change to match trends.

Truth stands on its own. The question is: Will you stand with it?

You Can't Redefine What You Didn't Create

If something's true today but false tomorrow, was it ever true to begin with?

That's not conviction. That's confusion.

Real truth is solid. It holds up under pressure.
It doesn't need applause to be real, and it doesn't disappear when people disagree.

When you **stand for something real**, you don't have to scramble to keep up with every new idea.

You already know where your feet are planted.

Real Teen Example – Ethan, 17, from Rapid City, South Dakota

In a group discussion, Ethan said he believed there's one truth, not "my truth" and "your truth." One student got offended. Another rolled their eyes. But Ethan stayed calm. "I'm not saying I know everything," he said. "I'm saying truth isn't up for redesign." Later, a classmate messaged him and said, "You said what I've been thinking, but I didn't know how." One voice, steady, made room for another.

Truth Doesn't Need Permission to Be True

The culture wants you to believe truth is flexible, like a playlist you can edit.
But the most freeing thing you'll ever discover is this:

You don't carry truth. It carries you.

Wisdom *doesn't invent truth, it recognizes it. In a world obsessed with reinvention, wisdom reminds us that some things should never be redesigned.*

When you let truth shape your identity, your decisions, your relationships, you don't have to guess who you are anymore.

And no trend can undo what's eternal.

Bold Defender – Jada, 16, from Cody, Wyoming

Jada was in a school club where everyone shared personal values. Most said things like, "I create my own truth." When it was her turn, she said, "I believe truth already exists, and it's my job to live up to it, not change it." The room got quiet. She wasn't rude. She was clear. Afterward, a teacher said, "That was the first real definition of truth I've heard all day."

✦ Your Takeaways

You don't invent truth.
You discover it.

You don't bend it to fit you.
You reshape yourself to follow it.

Because the world doesn't need more people making up their own version of reality.

It needs people who will **stand for something** that's already true.

"By their fruit you will recognize them..."
— *Matthew 7:16-20*

> 'I was seated in a crowded hall and I yelled, '*What is truth?*"—then ran out the back door, not wanting to hear the answer.
> —ANONYMOUS

Chapter 34: You're Not the Only One

Sometimes when you take a stand, it feels like no one else is with you.

You post something honest—crickets.
You speak up in class—awkward silence.
You stay home when everyone else is out—texts stop coming.

But you're not the only one.
You're part of a much bigger story.

Faith Doesn't Always Trend, But It Always Matters

What's right isn't always what's popular.
But it's **never without impact**.

You may not see it right away. But when you choose truth, someone else notices.
Someone else finds courage.
Someone else feels less alone.

And that ripple matters.

You're not just standing alone, you're standing **for something** that has **echoed through generations.**

Wisdom *sees beyond the moment. It reminds you that today's loneliness may become tomorrow's leadership because truth always outlasts trend.*

Real Teen Example – Aiden, 16, from Indiana

Aiden refused to join a group chat where classmates shared explicit images. When asked why, he simply said, "Because I want to respect people, not objectify them." He got mocked, but days later, another student privately thanked him. "I didn't want to be in it either, but I didn't know how to back out. You gave me a way." Aiden stood alone, but not for long.

Bold Defender Spotlight: Tim Tebow

Tim Tebow isn't just a former NFL quarterback or Heisman winner.
He's a man who's lived his faith **publicly and unapologetically**.

From writing Bible verses on his eye black to speaking about saving sex for marriage, he's faced mockery, media attacks, and skepticism from both sports and cultural circles.

But he never flinched.

"I don't want to be liked for who I'm not. I'd rather be disliked for who I am."

His boldness didn't come from arrogance, it came from **anchored identity.**

And it reminded millions that conviction doesn't make you weird.
It makes you **real.**

Another Bold Defender – Brielle, 17, from Arlington, Virginia

Brielle turned down a scholarship to a school that required students to sign a "values-neutrality" clause. "If I have to be silent about what I believe," she said, "then I'm not really free to learn." Her counselor warned she might not get another offer. But she did, and from a school that admired her stance. "You're the kind of student we want," they told her.

✦ Your Takeaways

You're not crazy.
You're not alone.
You're not outdated.

You are part of a growing group of teens and adults who refuse to bow to culture just to fit in.

When you stand for something that matters, you'll find others who do too. And together, you become unshakable.

Chapter 35: The Little Moments Count Most

Everyone talks about the big moments: the dramatic stands, the public speeches, the viral videos.
But most of your character isn't built in front of a crowd.

It's built in the **quiet**, when you think no one's paying attention.
When you're alone with a choice that matters.

And what you do then…
that's who you are.

Your Integrity Isn't Just Public, It's Personal

You might never stand on a stage.
But you will stand in front of a screen, a message, a moment where compromise would be easy.

Those are the moments that count.

Because they form your habits.
They shape your future.
They define the kind of person you're becoming, **not the one you pretend to be, but the one you actually are.**

That's why you need to **stand for something** even when no one's clapping for you.

Wisdom *is knowing not just what's right, but when and how to do it even when no one sees. It turns quiet choices into lasting character.*

Real Teen Example – Caleb, 15, from Columbus, Georgia
Caleb was hanging out with friends when someone pulled out a vape pen. They passed it around like it was nothing.

When it got to him, he said, "Nah, I'm good." Nobody yelled. Nobody pressured. But the moment still mattered because Caleb didn't explain or apologize. He just stood quietly on what he believed. One of his friends later said, "I kinda wish I'd done the same."

The Hidden Choices Build the Strongest Foundation

Think about the people you admire, not just the ones who are famous, but the ones you trust.
Why do you respect them?

It's not usually because of one big, flashy decision.
It's because of **consistent integrity over time**.

They show up.
They tell the truth.
They choose what's right when no one's watching.

And over time, **those small choices create a reputation you can't fake.**

The world might not notice right away, but your future will.

When you say no to a lie.
When you close the tab.
When you walk away instead of going along.
You're not just avoiding a mistake, you're building a life that stands.

Bold Defender – Taryn, 16, from Laconia, New Hampshire
Taryn was the only one in her group who didn't cheat on the take-home test. When the teacher found out, she asked the class who had been honest. Taryn raised her hand—alone. Some kids rolled their eyes. One even muttered, "Teacher's pet." But after class, the teacher said, "Thank you. It matters more than you know." Taryn didn't stand out to impress. She stood up because **truth mattered more than approval.**

✦ **Your Takeaways**

The world loves big performances.
But God watches the small, private moments that form the real you.

When you **stand for something** in the little things, you're building a life that can handle the big things.
Even when no one sees it, it still matters.

"We are what we repeatedly do. Excellence, then, is not an act but a habit."
— *Aristotle*

Chapter 36: Being Liked Is Overrated

We live in a world obsessed with likes, hearts, shares, and followers.
Your worth can feel like it's tied to a thumbs-up.
But here's the truth:

Being liked isn't the same as being right.
And being popular doesn't mean you're living with purpose.

The Danger of Chasing Approval

When you're focused on being liked, you start making quiet compromises:

- You stay silent when you should speak up.

- You laugh at something you know isn't funny just to blend in.

- You post things that get attention, even if they chip away at your integrity.

It doesn't happen all at once.
But slowly, your convictions start taking a back seat to your image.
And without even realizing it, you stop standing for something real because you're too busy standing where it's safe.

Popularity Fades, But Character Stays

Think about the people who were "cool" five years ago.
Most of them are forgotten.
But the people who lived with **honor**, **truth**, and **consistency**,

those are the ones others come back to for advice, for strength, for direction.

Being liked might feel good for a moment.
But being **trusted** and **respected**? That lasts.

Wisdom *is what reminds you that doing what's right will never be as loud as doing what's popular, but it matters more, and it lasts longer.*

When you care more about your character than your comments section, you become someone who's not just **seen**, but **counted on**.

Real Teen Example – Trinity, 16, from Fort Wayne, Indiana

Trinity lost friends when she started posting about her faith online. One told her, "You've changed. You think you're better now." Trinity didn't respond with drama. She posted a note to her story instead: "I've changed because truth changes people. I'm still me, just clearer." Months later, the same friend reached out during a tough season. "I don't have anyone to talk to. Can I ask you something about prayer?" Being liked was never the goal, being honest was.

You Can't Please Everyone. So Stop Trying

Here's the trap most people fall into:

You start saying what people want to hear.
You start doing what makes them smile.

You start avoiding anything that might cause tension even when it matters.

And before long, you're not standing for something anymore.

You're just **drifting,** trying to keep everyone happy, but losing track of who you really are.

The truth?
Trying to please everyone is the fastest way to lose your integrity.

Because you can't speak clearly and keep everyone comfortable.
You can't live with conviction and avoid every conflict.
You can't be brave and be bland at the same time.

If you live for applause, you'll die from silence.

Even Jesus, the most loving, perfect person who ever walked the earth, was misunderstood, criticized, rejected, and hated.
Not because He failed.
But because He told the truth with no apology and no compromise.

If that happened to Him, why would we expect to be treated better for doing the right thing?

There will be people who misjudge you.
Who twist your words.
Who call you names just to pressure you into silence.

Let them.

You weren't made to live under everyone else's approval.
You were made to live under truth.

You can't stand for something meaningful without making someone uncomfortable.
But that's not your failure. That's your faithfulness.

Bold Defender – Dylan, 17, from Shiloh, Tennessee
Dylan was the only one in his student council who voted against a campaign that promoted values he didn't believe in. His classmates called him a "bigot" and tried to push him off the team. He didn't fight back. He just calmly explained his convictions. One teacher pulled him aside afterward and said, "You handled that with more maturity than most adults." Dylan didn't need applause. He had **peace**.

✦ **Your Takeaways**

Being liked is easy.
Being consistent takes guts.

You weren't made to blend in.
You were made to **stand for something** even when it makes you stand out.

So let the crowd walk on.
You walk tall.

Chapter 37: Say the Hard Thing Anyway

It's easy to talk when everyone agrees with you.
It's harder when your words might make people uncomfortable, or even upset.

But silence isn't always kindness.
And truth isn't always soft.

Sometimes, the most loving thing you can do is speak up, **not to be cruel, but to be clear.**

Love Doesn't Hide the Truth

Our culture says, *"Don't offend."*
But Scripture says, *"Speak the truth in love."*

Stand for something.

That doesn't mean go looking for a fight.
It means don't **back down** when something needs to be said.

If someone's heading in the wrong direction, and you care about them, you won't stay quiet.
You'll risk the awkward moment to give them what they actually need: **honesty wrapped in compassion**.

That's not judgment.
That's courage.

Example #1 – Lucas, 17, from Frankfort, Kentucky

Lucas noticed his friend making destructive choices: partying, drinking, losing focus. He didn't shame him. He just said, "I don't think this is who you really are. I miss who you were last year." His friend blew up at first. But weeks later, he texted: "You were right. Nobody else had the guts to tell me." Truth cost Lucas a moment of peace, but saved his friend from going further off course.

You Can Be Honest Without Being Harsh

We've all seen it: someone blurts out the truth like a weapon, then shrugs and says,

"Just being honest."

But truth isn't a license to tear people down.
It's a tool, **and tools are meant to build, not break.**

You don't have to yell to be heard.
You don't have to embarrass someone to make a point.
You don't have to win the argument to be right.

Honesty with humility is one of the rarest forms of strength. Because it means you've chosen self-control over self-righteousness.

You pause before speaking, not out of fear, but out of care.
You choose words that cut through confusion, not character.

Being gentle doesn't make you weak.
It makes you *wise*.
It means you're not speaking to feel better about yourself.
You're speaking to help someone else see **what they need to see** even if it's uncomfortable.

Wisdom *isn't about knowing when to stay quiet, it's about knowing when to speak in a way that builds rather than breaks.*

Sometimes that means saying something no one else will. Other times, it means saying it in a way no one else has.

When you speak truth with love, your words become a gift, not a grenade.

Example #2 – Elise, 16, from Gettysburg, Pennsylvania
Elise was in a group chat where someone started mocking another girl from school. Everyone laughed. Elise didn't. She messaged the group: "This isn't cool. If this were about you, how would it feel?" The chat went silent. Some left the group. But one girl later messaged her privately: "Thanks for saying something. I didn't know how to." Elise didn't shame. She just spoke up with character.

✦ **Your Takeaways**

Telling the truth won't always win you applause.
Sometimes, it'll cost you comfort.

But if you want to **stand for something**, you can't stay silent when words need to be said.
Say it kindly. Say it clearly.
Say it anyway.

"Most people say that it is the intellect which makes a great scientist. They are wrong: it is character."
— *Albert Einstein*

Chapter 38: The Culture You're Built to Stand In

Scrolling Doesn't Shape You, Character Does

You spend hours a day looking at other people's lives. Perfect angles. Filtered faces. Highlight reels. It's easy to think that's where identity comes from: how you look, how you're liked, or how many people are watching.

But scrolling doesn't shape you. It distracts you.

Character doesn't come from curating your image. It comes from living your values.

It's not wrong to be online. It's not weak to want to be seen. But don't let the feed define you. Don't let comparison rewrite your story. Because what people post can never match what real character builds over time.

You weren't made to chase likes.
You were made to stand.

Strength Isn't Always Loud

Nobody sees your private battles. The stress you carry. The thoughts that spiral at night. The pressure to hold it together when everything feels like it's slipping.

Sometimes, strength is just getting out of bed.
Sometimes, it's staying quiet when your emotions are loud.
Sometimes, it's asking for help when your pride says don't.

You don't need to fake "fine." Real strength isn't found in pretending, it's found in perseverance. And character isn't about never struggling. It's about choosing truth, peace, and courage when fear would be easier.

You don't need to be fearless.
You just need to be faithful.

Digital Voices vs. Real Influence

The internet is loud.
Everyone has a platform. Everyone has an opinion.
But volume isn't the same as value.

It's easy to believe that influence means going viral, trending, or getting noticed. But the strongest voices aren't always the ones with the most followers. They're the ones people trust even when no one's watching.

Real influence isn't about how many people you reach.
It's about how deeply you reach them.

You don't need to go viral to matter. You don't need to trend to lead. The loudest person in the room isn't always the one people listen to when it counts.

Your life speaks louder than any post.
Let it say something that lasts.

Truth & Conviction in the Age of Spin

In today's world, truth feels like it's up for debate.
People twist it. Redefine it. Use it when it helps them, ignore it when it doesn't. But here's the thing: **truth doesn't change just because culture does.**

Wisdom *helps you filter the noise. It grounds you in truth when the world wants you confused.*

Conviction means standing for what's right *even when it's not trending*. It means refusing to trade what's true for what's easy.

It means you don't bend your beliefs to match the moment, you anchor them to something bigger, like the truth that doesn't change when your friends do, or the values that stay steady even when your feelings don't doesn't make you arrogant.

It makes you stable.

You don't have to shout your truth to prove it's real.
You just have to live it, consistently, even when it costs you.

You Are Not Alone

It might feel like you're the only one trying to live with conviction.
Like you're swimming upstream while everyone else floats with the current.

But you're not alone.
Every time you choose truth over trends, someone notices.
Every time you live with character, someone gains courage to do the same.

There are others quietly standing, quietly fighting, quietly refusing to give up who they are.

You may not see them.
They may not post about it.
But they're out there, just like you, choosing truth in a world that keeps pushing lies.

You're part of something bigger.
And what you do next might be the moment someone else decides to stand too.

Chapter 39: Don't Just Stand Here, Stand for Something

You've made it.
Thirty-nine chapters; 39 different ways to challenge the noise, think deeper, live louder, and be anchored in something that lasts.

Now it's your turn.

Not to read.
Not to scroll.
But to **live**.

Because truth isn't something you admire from a distance.
It's something you **act on**.

The World Doesn't Need More Performers

Every day, you're surrounded by people trying to say the right thing, post the right thing, perform the right thing, just to stay accepted.

But culture doesn't need more *safe performers*.
It needs **bold anchors**.

People who:

- Know what's right.

- Choose what's right.

- And stay grounded even when the wind picks up.

This world needs teens who are unshaken, not because they're loud, but because they're **clear**.

Wisdom *anchors courage. Without it, boldness becomes noise instead of strength.*

If you're waiting for the crowd to approve before you speak, you're already late.
If you're waiting for things to be easy before you do what's right, you'll never begin.

Real strength doesn't wait for permission.
It shows up with character and lets the results speak for themselves.

Real Courage Is Consistent, Not Loud

You don't have to preach on a stage or post a viral video.
You just have to **live with clarity when it's inconvenient**.

Courage is doing the right thing:

- When it costs you your seat at the table.

- When your friends roll their eyes.

- When the crowd goes one way and you feel the pull to follow.

Sometimes, courage means raising your hand.
Sometimes, it means walking away.
Other times, it means standing silently, but **standing firm**.

And while culture might reward the loudest voice in the room, **God honors the quiet strength of those who live by truth.**

Let that be you.

Let your life say something even when your mouth doesn't.
Let your integrity echo long after the noise fades.

Because when you consistently choose what's right, day after day, you become someone the world can count on, even when it doesn't clap for you.

✦ Your Takeaways

You don't need a platform to have a purpose.
You don't need popularity to make an impact.
You don't need the crowd to believe in you before you take a stand.

You just need the courage to do what you know is right—every time.

So here's the final challenge:
Don't just agree with this book.
Don't just highlight it, share it, or quote it.

Live it.

Every hallway.
Every group chat.
Every decision.
Every day.

Stand for something because the world is full of people who don't.

WHAT'S THE PURPOSE OF VALUES?

Here Are 7 Answers

1. GUIDANCE

Values help you make choices that align with what you believe is right and important. When faced with tough decisions, having clear values can guide you in making the best choices.

2. BUILDS CHARACTER
Values shape who you are as a person. They help you develop traits like honesty, kindness, and responsibility, which define your character and how others see you.

3. SET PRIORITIES

Values help you prioritize what matters most in your life. Whether it's family, education, or friendships, knowing your values helps you focus your time and energy on what's important.

4. IMPROVES RELATIONSHIPS
Sharing common values with friends and family strengthens your relationships. Values like respect, trust, and loyalty create a strong foundation for meaningful connections with others.

5. PROVIDES DIRECTION

Values give you a sense of direction and purpose. They help you set goals and stay motivated, knowing that what you're working towards is meaningful to you.

6. BUILDS CONFIDENCE

When you act according to your values, you feel more confident and self-assured. You know you're staying true to yourself, which boosts your self-esteem.

7. FOSTERS CARE

Values like fairness, empathy, and compassion contribute to making the world a better place. When you live by positive values, you help create a more just and caring community.

BOTTOM LINE
Having values is like having a personal compass that guides you through life, helping you become the best version of yourself and positively impact the world around you. It means developing your character, which can begin here.

Vital Chapter: How to Discover What You Stand For

(Before You're Asked to Defend It)

Throughout this book, you've "heard" it loudly and clearly: **Stand for something.**

But what if you're not sure what that *something* is?

What if no one's ever asked you to name your values?
What if you've never stopped long enough to figure them out?

That's what this chapter is for.

Because it's not enough to feel inspired.
You need to know what you believe and why.

Step 1: Know What You Believe, Not Just What You've Been Told

It's easy to borrow beliefs from parents, teachers, or influencers.
But when life turns up the pressure, secondhand convictions won't hold.

You need to ask:

- *Do I believe this because it's true, or because it's familiar?*
- *Would I still believe this if it cost me popularity?*
- *Am I building my life on this—or just repeating it out loud?*

Real conviction starts when your beliefs become personal—*not just inherited.*

Step 2: Define What Values Matter Most

Think about the kind of person you want to be.
Then ask: *What values will get me there?*

Here's a list to help you reflect:

- **Generosity** – Giving freely of time, help, or resources. Seen in everything from charity work to neighbors lending a hand.

- **Empathy** – Understanding and caring about others' feelings and experiences. Key to kindness, service, and unity.

- **Self-Reliance** – Believing in your ability to solve problems and take responsibility without always depending on others.

- **Kindness** – Doing good without being asked. Builds trust and brings people together.

- **Gratitude** – Appreciating what you have and recognizing the efforts of others.

- **Integrity** – Doing what's right even when it's hard, unpopular, or invisible.

- **Perseverance** – Not giving up when things get hard. Rooted in the pioneer and immigrant spirit.

- **Respect** – Treating others with dignity, even when they're different from you.

- **Accountability** – Owning your actions, both the wins and the mistakes.

- **Compassion** – Not just feeling for others, but stepping in to help.

- **Service** – Putting others first, especially in families, communities, or through military or civic roles.

- **Humility** – Being confident without needing attention; knowing your worth without boasting.

- **Courage** – Facing fear, challenge, or pressure with strength and purpose even when it's hard or unpopular.

- **Responsibility** - owning your actions and following up on what you're supposed to do

- **Honesty** - being sincere and transparent, it'd telling the truth

- **Conviction** – Holding firmly to what's right, even when you're alone or misunderstood.

Circle the ones that hit hardest.
Then write down your top **five**. These are your **core values**, your internal compass.

Step 3: Test It Against God's Word

Feelings change.
Culture shifts.
Even your friends might push you to compromise.

That's why your values need a stronger foundation than emotion.

Ask:

- *What does Scripture say about these values?*

- *Do they reflect God's truth, or just my comfort?*

- *Am I open to correction if I find I've built on the wrong thing?*

If you want to stand tall, you need roots that don't move.

Step 4: Talk With People You Respect

Who do you admire, not just on a screen, but in real life?

Ask them:

- *What values have shaped your life the most?*
- *Was there ever a time you had to stand alone for what you believed?*
- *What would you tell your younger self about staying grounded?*

Wisdom is everywhere. You just have to ask for it.

Elderly people are a terrific source because they have so many years of accumulated wisdom, and they're only too happy to share.

Step 5: Practice Before It's Popular

The real test doesn't happen when everything's easy.
It happens when your values are on the line.

That's why you need to rehearse your courage *before* the crowd shows up.

Try this:

- Write down your 5 core values on the worksheet that follows.
- For each one, write a sentence about what it looks like in action.
- Picture a situation where you might have to defend it and decide now how you'll respond.

You don't rise to the level of your intentions.
You rise to the level of your **preparation**.

✦ Your Takeaways

This isn't about being perfect.
It's about being **clear**.

Because when the pressure hits, it's too late to figure out what you stand for.
By then, you'll either **stand firm,** or fall into whatever everyone else is doing.

So define it. Own it. **Live it.**

Don't just stand here.

Stand for something.

I didn't write this book from the sidelines. I've taken my own stand: for truth that doesn't shift, for faith that doesn't flinch, and for character that still counts. In a world that keeps telling you to blend in, I chose to speak up. This is what I stand for. Now it's your turn.

> **WHY YOU DON'T SEE 'TRUTH' IN THE LIST OF VALUES**
>
> You might wonder why 'Truth' isn't listed alongside the other values in this book.
>
> That's because Truth isn't just a value—Truth is a Person.
>
> Jesus didn't say, "I know the truth." He said, "I am the Truth." (John 14:6).
>
> To reduce Truth to a character trait would be like calling the sun just another lightbulb.
>
> Every other value in this book—courage, humility, integrity, perseverance—only has meaning because they're built on Him.

WORKSHEET — To Help You Discover Your Values
What Do You Stand For?

Use these two pages to help you identify and clarify your core values. When pressure hits, this page will help you remember what matters most.

Step 1: Dig Deep
Answer these honestly:
- Do I believe this because it's true, or because it's familiar?
- Would I still believe this if it cost me popularity or comfort?
- Can I explain this value in my own words?

Step 2: Choose Your Top 5 Values
Circle or highlight your top 5:

Courage	Respect
Conviction	Gratitude
Self-Control	Compassion
Honesty	Loyalty
Responsibility	Perseverance
Humility	Service
Accountability	Faith
Generosity	Self-reliance

Step 3: Define What They Mean to You
For each value you selected, describe what it looks like in your life:

1. _____

   What it means to me:
   _____

   How I plan to live this out:
   _____

2. _____

   What it means to me:
   _____

   How I plan to live this out:
   _____

3. _____

   What it means to me:
   _____

   How I plan to live this out:
   _____

4. _____

   What it means to me:
   _____

   How I plan to live this out:
   _____

5. _____

   What it means to me:
   _____

   How I plan to live this out:
   _____

Step 4: Prepare to Stand
Picture a moment when it might be hard to live by your values. What will you do?

Write out your plan:

_____

_____

_____

_____

The 7-Day Stand-For-Something Challenge

Day 1 – Tell the Truth Anyway
Even if it's awkward. Even if it costs you.
Speak up today—honestly and kindly—when you'd usually stay quiet or hide the truth.

Day 2 – Listen All the Way Through
Put down your phone. Look them in the eye. Don't interrupt.
Today, listen like it matters because it does.

Day 3 – Stand Alone If You Have To
You don't need the crowd to do what's right.
If something's off, say no even if you're the only one who does.

Day 4 – Say the Hard Thing (With Respect)
Truth doesn't have to be loud, but it has to be clear.
Today, don't sugarcoat what matters. Speak with courage and kindness.

Day 5 – Choose Quiet Over Clout
You don't have to prove anything to anyone.
Take a break from seeking likes or validation. Let your peace be enough today.

Day 6 – Be Bold With Your "Yes"
Don't just say no to pressure, say yes to purpose.
Say yes to something that empowers you, helps someone, or honors who you are.

Day 7 – Lift Someone Else Up|
Character isn't self-centered. Text someone encouragement. Apologize. Show up. Serve quietly.

Real character isn't built in one moment. It's built in many small ones. Start here and keep going.

So, after 7 days, what did you learn?
What was hard? What's your next stand?

The 16 Values: Historical and Biblical Roots

Courage
Historical: Ancient Greece, Patrick Henry, cardinal virtues
Biblical: Joshua 1:9 – "Be strong and courageous... for the Lord your God is with you."

Integrity
Historical: American Revolution, Washington's honesty
Biblical: Proverbs 10:9 – "Whoever walks in integrity walks securely."

Perseverance
Historical: Underground Railroad, WWII home front
Biblical: Romans 5:3–4 – "Suffering produces perseverance; perseverance produces virtue, and virtue hope."

Respect
Historical: Native American traditions, civic respect
Biblical: 1 Peter 2:17 – "Show proper respect to everyone."

Accountability
Historical: John Adams on power & responsibility
Biblical: Romans 14:12 – "Each of us will give an account of ourselves to God."

Compassion
Historical: Florence Nightingale, Clara Barton
Biblical: Colossians 3:12 – "Clothe yourselves with compassion, kindness, humility, gentleness, and patience."

Kindness
Historical: Abraham Lincoln's personal reputation
Biblical: Ephesians 4:32 – "Be kind and compassionate to one another."

Gratitude
Historical: First Thanksgiving, Washington's 1789 Proclamation
Biblical: 1 Thessalonians 5:18 – "Give thanks in all circumstances."

Generosity
Historical: Andrew Carnegie's philanthropy
Biblical: 2 Corinthians 9:6 – "Whoever sows generously will also reap generously."

Humility
Historical: Lincoln's humility in leadership
Biblical: Philippians 2:3 – "'In humility value others above yourselves."

Service
Historical: Peace Corps, civic duty traditions
Biblical: Mark 10:45 – "The Son of Man did not come to be served, but to serve."

Self-Reliance
Historical: Ralph Waldo Emerson's essay Self-Reliance
Biblical: Galatians 6:5 – "For each one should carry their own load."

Empathy
Historical: Harriet Beecher Stowe's influence
Biblical: Romans 12:15 – "Rejoice with those who rejoice; mourn with those who mourn."

Conviction
Historical: Martin Luther, MLK Jr., moral courage
Biblical: 1 Corinthians 16:13 – "Stand firm in the faith; be courageous; be strong."

Honesty
Historical: Honest Abe, Washington folklore
Biblical: Proverbs 12:22 – "The Lord delights in people who are trustworthy."

Faith
Historical: Early Christian martyrs, American spiritual revivals
Biblical: Hebrews 11:1 – "Faith is confidence in what we hope for and assurance about what we do not see."

These values are introduced earlier in the *Stand For Something™ Values Series,* beginning with a reflective coloring book for younger readers, ages 7-12.

Bibliography

1. **Frankl, Viktor E.** *Man's Search for Meaning*. Beacon Press, 2006.

    - A classic work on finding meaning in life, even in the most difficult circumstances, written by a Holocaust survivor and psychiatrist. It's especially relevant for those searching for a sense of purpose.

2. **Pew Research Center.** *The Future of World Religions: Population Growth Projections, 2010-2050*. Pew Research Center, 2015.

    - Provides statistical data on the rise of secularism and religious trends worldwide, relevant for understanding the shifts in belief systems and their impact on society.

3. **Prager, Dennis.** *The Ten Commandments: Still the Best Moral Code*. Regnery Publishing, 2015.

    - An exploration of the Ten Commandments and how they continue to offer timeless wisdom for navigating modern moral dilemmas.

4. **Trueman, Carl R.** *The Rise and Triumph of the Modern Self: Cultural Amnesia, Expressive Individualism, and the Road to Sexual Revolution*. Crossway, 2020.

    - A deep dive into the rise of expressive individualism and how it has reshaped modern culture, helping explain the rise of secularism and relativism.

5. **Schwarz, Gene.** *The Big Idea: Focus the Message, Multiply the Impact*. Howard Books, 2007.

    o   A book on the importance of clarity and focus when communicating important ideas. Useful for understanding how to deliver truth effectively to today's audience.

6. **Schaeffer, Francis A.** *The God Who Is There*. IVP Books, 2000.

    o   A foundational work that addresses the rise of secularism and offers a Christian perspective on the importance of truth and worldview.

7. **Smith, Christian, and Melinda Lundquist Denton.** *Soul Searching: The Religious and Spiritual Lives of American Teenagers*. Oxford University Press, 2005.

    o   Explores the state of religion and spirituality among teens, providing insights into how the younger generation is responding to cultural and religious shifts.

8. **Harris, Joshua.** *I Kissed Dating Goodbye: A New Attitude Toward Relationships and Romance*. Multnomah Books, 1997.

    o   Though primarily about relationships, this book focuses on the importance of biblical values in shaping one's identity and purpose in a culture that often disregards those values.

9. **Crouch, Andy.** *Culture Making: Recovering Our Creative Calling*. InterVarsity Press, 2008.

    o   A work that encourages Christians to engage actively with culture, offering insights on how to **reshape** culture for good, not simply **resist** or **retreat** from it.

10. **Barna, George.** *Generation Z: Their Voices, Their Lives.* Barna Group, 2018.

- A study on Generation Z and their worldview, providing insight into the challenges facing today's youth and their evolving attitudes toward faith, truth, and morality.

11. **Haidt, Jonathan.** *The Anxious Generation.* 2024.

- Explores how smartphones and social media have contributed to the rise in mental health issues among adolescents, advocating for changes in parenting and education to mitigate these effects.

12. **Weinstein, Emily, and Carrie James.** *Behind Their Screens.* 2022.

- Delves into the complexities of teen digital lives, offering a nuanced understanding of teen behavior online, and how they are engaging with the digital world.

13. **Hari, Johann.** *Stolen Focus: Why You Can't Pay Attention.* Bloomsbury, 2022.

- A critical look at how modern technology and social media have eroded our attention spans, with particular focus on its effects on young people.

14. **Homayoun, Ana.** *Social Media Wellness: Helping Tweens and Teens Thrive in an Unbalanced Digital World.* 2022.

- Provides strategies for fostering healthy online habits and emotional well-being for teens and tweens in an era dominated by social media.

16. **Dreisbach, Daniel.** *Reading the Bible with the Founding Fathers.* 2017.

- Explores how the Bible shaped the political thinking of America's founders, documenting its influence on their language, moral reasoning, and public discourse.

17. Sax, Leonard, *The Collapse Of Parenting,* How We Hurt Our Kids...Basic Books, 2015.

· _____

Acknowledgements

All graphics in this book were designed by ChatGPT.

Scripture quotations taken from The Holy Bible, New International Version®, NIV®. Copyright ©1973, 1978, 1984, 2011 by Biblica, Inc.™ Used by permission. All rights reserved worldwide.

> "Everyone who hears these words of mine and puts them into practice is like a wise man who built his house on the rock."
>
> Matthew 7:24

Appendix: A Note to Homeschool Families & Church Leaders

Stand For Something was written for one purpose:
To help teens build **unshakable character** in a culture that constantly pushes compromise.

Whether you're a parent, small group leader, youth pastor, or homeschool instructor, this book gives you a tool to guide students toward **truth, clarity, and conviction without being preachy or outdated.**

How to Use This Book in Your Setting

- **1–2 Chapters a Week**
  Each chapter is short and discussion-ready. Teens can read independently or as a group.

- **Use the 2 Discussion Questions on Page 17**
  Perfect for group settings or one-on-one mentoring.

- **Optional Weekly Focus**
  Pair each week's reading with one small challenge: a journal reflection, a conversation at home, or a real-life "stand-up" moment.

- **Use the 7-Day Challenge as a Wrap-Up**
  After the book is finished, the 7-Day Self-Exam can help teens apply what they've learned in their daily choices.

Why This Book Works in Homes and Churches

- It's grounded in biblical values, but speaks in the language teens actually understand.

- It avoids lectures and delivers truth through stories, clarity, and reflection.

- It empowers both leaders and learners; *you don't have to prepare lessons. Just show up and engage.*

Final Encouragement

Teens don't need hype.
They need hope.
And they need **leaders who are anchored** so they can become anchored, too.

This book is your starting point. The conversation it sparks is where the change begins.

Topical Index: Where to Find What Matters

Approval & People-Pleasing
– The Trap of Needing Approval (p.45)
– You Don't Need Everyone to Like You (p.96)
– Don't Trade Clarity for Acceptance (p.99)
– Being Liked Is Overrated (p.118)

Authenticity & Identity
– The Struggle for Authenticity (p.23)
– You're Not Who They Say You Are (p.103)
– You're Not the Only One (p.112)
– The Lie of "Just Be Yourself" (p.18)

Boundaries & Saying No
– The Importance of Boundaries (p.32)
– The Power of Saying "No" (p.36)
– Don't Confuse Freedom With Chaos (p.84)

Character
– The Strength of Character (p.26)
– Courage Isn't Loud, But It's Real (p.74)
– Courage Isn't Loud Either (p.97)
– Say the Hard Thing Anyway (p.122)

Courage & Conviction
– The Courage to Speak Up (p.27)
– Choosing Conviction Over Comfort (p.54)
– Conviction Isn't Hate (p.93)
– You Can Be Bold Without Being Loud (p.107)

Digital Culture & Comparison
– What You Laugh At, You Learn From (p.72)
– The Culture You're Built to Stand In (p.125)

Faith & Truth
– The Power of Truth (p.21)
– When Truth Isn't Popular (p.51)
– You Don't Create Truth, You Align With It (p.105)
– Truth Isn't Trendy, And That's The Point (p.87)
– The World's Approval Isn't Worth Your Soul (p.75)

Loneliness & Standing Alone
– Standing When You Feel Alone (p.48)
– Standing Alone Without Feeling Alone (p.66)
– Opposition Doesn't Mean You're Wrong (p.105)

Voice & Silence
– The Risk of Staying Silent (p.38)
– Strength Isn't Always Loud (p.65)
– Don't Just Stand There, Stand For Something (p.122)

"Christian ideas were to a significant degree responsible for the American founding."

Mark David Hall
American Historian

'The Bible was the most frequently cited source in the political literature of the American founding era.

Daniel L. Dreisbach
Professor of American Legal History

This Dreisbach quote comes from his research into the intellectual influences on America's founders, particularly his analysis of political writings between 1760 and 1805. In Dreisbach's work, especially in *Reading the Bible with the Founding Fathers*, he emphasizes that **biblical themes, such as covenant, justice, and moral law, deeply informed the political thinking of the era**, often more than Enlightenment sources alone.

About The Author

Paul Lloyd Hemphill is an author, speaker, graphic designer, videographer, and a veteran with a deep commitment to helping America's youth build character in a culture that's lost its moral compass. With backgrounds in philosophy, theology, and media, he's spent decades asking the hard questions and crafting messages that make truth personal.

He has written twelve books, narrated four audiobooks, and produced a national video-based character education series, **America's 52 Stories**, for schools and families. His work focuses on one idea: helping teens believe in themselves and their country by demonstrating the power of character.

He's been a frequent TV guest, a strong voice for patriotism, and a relentless advocate for young people who search for meaning and support.

Paul received the Bronze Star Medal in Vietnam, not for valor, but for meritorious service. His commanding officer noted that he consistently went "above and beyond" in the performance of his daily duties. Oftentimes people just assume the medal was awarded for heroism. Paul always corrects them.

*"Letting that impression stand would feel like I was engaging in that shameful and undeserved label of **'stolen valor.'** No. I didn't earn it that way."*

He earned it by quietly doing more than his duties required, the kind of effort only a good leader would notice.

Paul's quiet correction says everything. Character means telling the truth, even when, as Paul says, *"it would cost me the kind of praise I didn't earn."*

Paul lives in Southborough, Massachusetts, with his wife, Ann Marie. They have two sons, John and Mark, and three grandchildren—Lyla, Anya, and Mason—and a family legacy that's being built one truth at a time.

Get the 3-volume series, BOLD DEFENDERS:

It's designed to inspire teens, parents, and educators by telling the true stories of individuals who have demonstrated exceptional character, courage, and conviction under pressure. Each volume dives into the lives of those who have boldly stood for what's right, even when it wasn't easy, and how those examples can shape the next generation.

Volume 1: **Stand For Something**
How to Live by Conviction When Culture Keeps Changing

- Focuses on **16 core faith-based values** like truth, responsibility, humility, and perseverance

- Features true stories of individuals who chose to live with integrity despite cultural pressure

- Includes **reflection questions** to guide teens and parents in applying the values to real life

Volume 2: **America's Bold 52**
True Stories of Americans Who Stood Strong When Others Stayed Silent

- Showcases **51 stories** (Are you the **52nd?**) of Americans who today stand for their beliefs and willingly take the heat

- Each story highlights key character traits that help these individuals **make a lasting impact**

- Perfect for **classroom or family discussions** about leadership and moral strength

Volume 3: **Profiles In Character**
A powerful blend of true stories from history and modern-day role models who stood firm in what they believed, often at a young age.

This volume equips teens to recognize what matters, who they're becoming, and how to live with conviction in a world that constantly shifts.

- Highlights real-life boldness from both the **past and present**

- Shows how **lasting character begins early** and sticks for life

- Offers **practical takeaways and reflection tools** for personal growth

When today's culture doesn't care about values, this book helps readers stand strong with their own.

Why Choose The Series, *Bold Defenders?*

It's how character is built.

Get One Free Video + One Free Graphic Every Week for 52 Weeks—No Credit Card. No Catch.

Watch the timeless values in this book come alive each week with free videos and colorful graphics inspired by powerful true stories from the most written-about event in America's past. Make values real for your family—one week at a time.

Use these videos with this book for a deeper family experience. | Sign up for the free videos at AmericanEducationDefenders.org

www.ingramcontent.com/pod-product-compliance
Lightning Source LLC
LaVergne TN
LVHW020931090426
835512LV00020B/3307